Manuscript

Who is this person?

Ali Mazhin

Who is this Person?

Who is this Person?

by
Ali Mazhin

N2
Print

Who is this Person?
By Ali Mazhin
Published by New Age World Publishing
ISBN: 1-59405-071-6

Dedication

This book is dedicated to all my friends who have stood by me. I won't mention names, but you know who you are. If you don't already know, I truly value all of these friendships.

My parents, mom and dad, I don't know of any other two parents who could deal with my madness and stay as beautiful and good as you guys are today.

My psychiatrist, you are one of the best. All my childhood friends and parents of friends, you don't know how much you mean to me.

To all the Iranians and everyone I know in Iran, *zende bush* (live) and to the girls that I've known, you make the world go round.

To all my teachers throughout school and my classmates, I express a thank you for sticking through with me.

I'll always remember the homeless people hanging in there, mental patients and the doctors that I've met.

And to all the good people – you are what keep me sane.

Peace

Contents

Introduction

To whom it may concern:

"There's always been crazy people, you just never hear about them." My name is Ali Mazhin, and I'm here to tell you about one. I'm worse off than Linda Blair in *The Exorcist.* I have chosen a life that is filled with pain. Drama is constant, and as much as I have tried to change, my soul is still imperfect and empty. I am a blank slate.

I don't know how I made it this far (23 years). I don't know how I will make it the rest of my life. Who am I? No-body. What am I? I do not know. I was raised in a rich family and surrounded by good people all throughout my life, but I say, "Screw them – I'd rather do nothing." It is a mental illness, an illness that I hate, and that I will overcome. I will come out a good man and a motivated person, with money.

I say and do nothing all day, never feeling like a true human being. I live like a normal happy person, but instead of happiness I feel hate. And as much as that happy person is depressed, I'm happy. I live and strive off madness. I'm a walking serial killer who has never actually killed anyone physically, and never will. From what I can remember, my head has images of events more interesting than ones explained in any novel. Most of them never happened, I'm told they're fantasies, delusions. But many people have told me they are real.

It's all something I'm not supposed to know about. I'm a fool, an actual fool, and I'm going to overcome that---a fool who sees the world with the sun coming down, and eyes wandering everywhere, painfully trying to interpret things. I feel homeless at 23. I have homeless people laugh at me with my reality. I'm a soldier, a soldier that never gives up and will live to see everyone else's lives grow. I guess Charles Darwin missed one.

I'm a hero to be alive and I vow to always have a roof over my head. Happiness, "ha, ha, ha," is what people say when they know me. The darkness that I've seen would be unbearable for the average person. Today I'm back to reality, I graduated from college, and am writing this in hopes to be rich and give some inspiration to anyone who thinks of suicide. I'm recalling most of my "so called: insane experiences. Inside I don't want to be happy; I am normal but playing a game—one that makes me laugh for what I have done. It is a way of winning. In this book are samples of my writings; they are disturbing.

In a sense, I am the dumbest person in the whole world. I have the attention span of three seconds, like a fish. Trust me, anyone can make it through college. I live the life of a fish out of water, constantly in conflict with myself, searching for water, never being myself. I must learn to love myself before I can be happier and be a friend to anyone. I'm meant to jump in the ocean and be with the fish. I'm savior of the human race. If I killed myself there would be peace on Earth, and people would be happier. But the lives I hold in my hands right now are large. Suicide for me would mean a lot of people would also give up after knowing me.

Love is the most important thing to me, and to most people. Because of it nobody could ever find a way to kill me. I've toyed with the human race and the boundaries of love. Yes, I want to think I'm special, but who doesn't? No, I am not special, but confused about my sexuality. The doctors say I'm straight. Nothing makes me happy. I could go gay and be happier, but if I'm truly not gay then what's the point? If there is one thing I've learned it's that there is nothing wrong with being gay. I've given gay people a very bad name because of my sexual conduct as a child. I have tried everything except for being Ali.

I have caused earthquakes; when the pain becomes unbearable, when I try to hide it for a long time, the Earth below me will start to shake. Sometimes after a hard day my bed will start to shake. Sometimes after a hard day my bed will shake as I try to fall asleep. If I'm in a dreary mood at school my desk sometimes uncontrollably shakes with other people using it. On a really bad day, the walls around me will attempt to collapse. The surf will sometimes rise also. I cannot do this at will. It doesn't happen too often.

I have been the most powerful man in the world, more powerful than the President of the United States. At one time I held a countless number of lives in my hands. If I were to commit suicide, the world would stop for a moment. My best friend, the person that I have come closest to, is going to be given the Presidency at 35 for the potential lost lives he saved in keeping me under control. This is most likely a delusion, as everyone tells me, and it probably is, but delusions seem so real that psychologists don't even try to argue whether they happened or not. The 1998 NBA lockout occurred because of my antics as a young kid.

I have never had a place on Earth, sinners never do, and I have no place on planet Mars. I can't be by other people too long. I am rarely comfortable with myself. No one knows how I could live with myself. I'm like a time bomb. It is conceivable that I am savior of the human race, but that we'll never know unless there's an afterlife. My sole purpose in life is to control the population, but that we'll never know unless there's an afterlife. My sole purpose in life is to control the population, but now it won't happen. I choose to live. Why? No one knows. Some of the smartest people in the world have analyzed me, to predict my behavior, however, I am not supposed to know about it. Numerous songs, and movies have been made about me.

What do I want? I want power. I want to feel what it is like to be special, a ruler. What does the future hold? No one knows, but all I can do now is smile and that will be my medicine to get through this. There is a good person inside of me and I strive to be him. Who is Ali? Everyone says, "He's crazy. All these writings are delusions of grandeur," and for all I know, they are. I have a very mild case of schizophrenia. My life is a joke. The truth is the events may or may have not happened in real life, but nonetheless they have happened in real life, but nonetheless they have happened one way of another in my mind. My writings are of the sexual stories that stand out the most.

Chapter 1

I was born in Tehran, Iran in 1978. After the first few months of my life, my parents decided to move to Bloomington, Indiana where I would be raised. My first vivid memory was somewhere between one and two. I remember lying on a blanket, faced up, lined up with other babies by my side. I instantly felt I was different. The whole world already seemed distorted. I looked around at the other babies and felt as though I was missing something. I was an actor already.

There was female nurse on duty. She was checking, overlooking the babies, as a nanny would do to make sure they are all right. I saw her laugh and play with a baby next to me. The baby naturally giggled as he or she was being played with. She gave the child joy. The nurse approached me with a smile and tried to play with me. I tried but couldn't genuinely laugh with her. My eyes just wandered around as if I was being played with. I didn't know what to look at. I couldn't connect with her on a normal level. I had known a few basic words, and could come up with a little thought. If only I could give you a sample of what goes on in my head you'd be amazed at how I can live through this.

She looked into my eyes, and the first thing I thought was, *Is this real? Why is she looking into my eyes? Why is she here?* I didn't feel there was a reason for anything to happen. *What the hell is going on?* I was already suffering, "I have this thing in my head," is what I murmured to her, as I pointed to the side of my head. This "thing" I was referring to is like a beam, setting barriers to keep me from developing meaning to everything, and causing every situation to be a new one. I had a beam of nothingness in my head; it blocked out thoughts and beliefs from being tangible. I guess in a sense one could say I'm really happy for not being able to think anything. But enjoying myself would make me a vegetable. I could try real hard and have thoughts come through, but it was nobody, just a physical being occupying space. I had a sense that the people around me did not have beams in their heads.

The nurse responded, "He could be gay." Supposedly there are a few gay people with a "thing" in their head that genetically constitutes their sexuality. This however is rare. I was afraid; I couldn't see a purpose to live, in the future, not even ten minutes. For a glimpse, I felt the sense of reality around me, and it felt good, like life was fun. However, it took effort to experience it, and it quickly faded. It looked so natural for everyone around me to experience it. I felt like my life would be a constant battle with little satisfaction. The nurse had a worried look on her face, as if she didn't know what to do with me.

I wanted to stop the confusion, *Yeah I'm gay*. I didn't want to be labeled crazy. I thought being gay made me handicapped.

"He's crazy," she said.

It's not that I knew exactly what she meant, but I could sense something unusual was going on. Something was wrong; this is a glimpse at the rest of my life, absolute chaos and suffering endured by all. I grasped for life, tying to make meaning and I began to hate myself with a passion. How could I like myself with a passion? How could I like myself if I'm crazy? It like looking at a homeless man enjoying himself. The very idea is disturbing to me. I felt that something bad was going to happen to me, but I didn't know what.

"We have to kill him," she said to a co-worker.

I then looked around at a few doctors doing their normal tasks, and thought of how happy they were with existence. How beautiful it is to be human. I began to believe what a wonderful thing life was, and I could only observe. Doctors were doing their job with a smile and the idea of work was not a bad thing.

The nurse approached me with some kind of device to end my life. I sensed what she was going to do. The reality around me made me feel uncomfortable. I had to stop it. I had to say the word, "No." I had to resist. The resistance became stronger and stronger. The nurse was just above me and pointed her device to kill me. I made squeamish movement and tried to find a way to resist. I really didn't even care if she injected me because I knew my life would be hard, but I felt there was nothing else to do at that moment so why not resist? "No!" I yelled.

She thought nothing of it, so did I, and she came closer to inject me when I thought, *I might as well say it again because it was fun,* "No," I said. Although it was negative, I felt a little bit of life.

She pulled back powerless, "Oh no, he's evil." I was confused as to where this was all going. "I was afraid a day like this would come, I have feared it for a long time."

She then turned to another doctor and told him to administer the killing. He agreed to do it because he thought he could, since he was stronger than the woman.

I felt special, and unusual kind of happiness, for a second, which a lot of schizophrenic's experience, thinking the disease they have is a good one. It was a sense of happiness that entailed a deep love between him and I.

"You can administer this! Look at you!" I pointed and smiled regarding him as a person. This is what makes me gay. The deep love I have for some people. Very few are woman.

"I love this guy," he said with a smile. I knew I could connect with people in a different way than normal, and I loved the power of granting silly love. It's like in *The Exorcist* how Linda Blair gives her illness to the exorcist at the end when he tries to physically kill her. She gets better in the end. However, in my case, when I give my illness to someone it still stays in me.

"I can't do this, have someone else try it."

Two or three other doctors unsuccessfully attempted to kill me. I felt good knowing they wouldn't overpower me, and at the same time horrible for doing it, because it's silly. I became a fish out of water, trying desperately to grasp for life at all times with the intelligence of a fish. All I did for many years is grasp for air. My life could be taken by only one person, me. I have the intelligence only to detect love. Love in the sense of what I mean to someone. I'm a blank slate, every person's dream, someone to love unconditionally. The *tabula rasa* theory is wrong I think. It states that everyone is born a blank slate and your personality is learned through experience. Could I still be a blank slate at 23? People are born with thoughts and attributed that make them human.

What is it? I thought, *Why aren't I normal? What can I do to make me feel normal?* I was let out of the hospital against her will, and the people in the hospital thought I would forget this early childhood experience; that I would recover, and as a normal person, pursue happiness. I would do things that made me happy. This is our sole purpose in being here. But this could not be, the reality of my life was different from the reality that most other people have.

To other people who didn't know me well I acted normal as a kid, and I could very well blend in and live a normal life, but the other people who knew me best thought differently. This thought was beginning to get into my head. Why do I have to struggle to make conversation, while I see other people talking, and laughing away, as though it were instrumental? Happiness is not instrumental, it requires effort, and when I give effort I am happier, but in a different way. Life seemed so fun for others, while I felt no true joy out of life, no compassion towards my fellow man. I knew I was different. I was no-body. But what could this difference do, what does it mean, what does it hold for the future, and what am I here for?

One day it all started over. I was with a group of five adults, ranging from the ages of 20-30, and we were talking. I did not feel natural with my talking. It was fake, only to buy extra time to live. I felt misplaced in every social situation. Finally, I blurted out in a curious and lovable voice, "What am I?"

They all laughed and one said with joyous intent, "Well, what are you thinking?" As one of the people in the group was talking. I sensed confidence, and a cocky attitude. It seemed as though he did not have any problems.

"Well, I like this guy."

"Ah," they all started laughing, and then there I forever thought of myself as shit. They were laughing at me. "There are words that describe you," they said, as though I was a freak.

"Like what?" I said in a demanding voice; I wanted to know who I was.

"Gay," one said, and they all laughed. *Oh shit, now what is life worth if people are going to look down at me?*

I turned to one person and said, "What are you thinking?"

"I'm thinking of the weather!" With astonishment, as if to say, "How stupid are you?"

"Jesus!" I said, "Look at you." I thought I was dealing with a brilliant man. When in reality, he was a normal person, who thinks of things. I thought that my problem was that I was gay, and I wasn't as good as everyone else. I had a handicap. "What are other names for gay people?" I asked.

They all laughed, "Queer, fag, homo, fruit."

"What does that mean?" I asked.

"Well that means that you like men." From all of this I was infuriated. *What me?* I thought, I wanted from the beginning of my life for it to be legendary, a life of a king, a prophet. And with this gay talk and all the laughing I said, "So gay people are the worse kind of people on this planet."

"No," they laughed. "There is nothing wrong with it." Boom, I could hear some insensitivity in the confident guy's voice, as if gays were inferior to a person like him. Like he was a "better" person. It hit me harder; *I'm the worse person in the world.* My life now meant nothing; I felt I no longer had a purpose. "So, what is the worse word in the world?"

"What!" they laughed in confusion.

I repeated, "What is the worse word in the world?"

"Asshole," one blurted laughing.

"Fuck," one said.

Finally, with hate one person says, "Shit."

To me, this sounded like the worst word in the English language. So, I now felt I was shit. "So, what do gay people do?" I asked.

"They suck each other's dicks," one laughed, as if where does this kid come up with these questions? I felt as though I was to do something, for I thought I was gay. I pointed to the confident straight guy, and said, "Can I suck your dick?" I knew it wasn't the right thing to say, but I said it.

"No" he said laughing. "I can never be happy" is what I later said. "I can never be happy," I said again in sorrow. "Well, Okay kid, but you're the only one," So I performed the act and the first thing I said was, "You're gay!" He was in disbelief that such a thing has been said. He laughed, and liked me.

"What's this kid going to become?" is what they all said. They were amazed that such an incident just happened. This kid was definitely the most unique character each of these people had ever met. I felt happy for a split second, and then delved into myself, and what I thought was, "You're shit!" I yelled.

"Oh no," is what that person said, "I can't like you."

"Why not?" I said.

"Because I like myself!" he said bluntly. At that time, I felt that I was better than that person, and I had adrenaline running though my veins, and for the first time in my life, truly felt alive. I killed him, not physically but mentally. Everyone had a look of shock and disbelief.

"Oh no," another person said, "You are going to ruin the world."

I felt special. I had some sort of power. Everyone had distressed looks.

"Kid, go kill yourself."

"Me kill myself? But why? I said. I shook my head no. I didn't want to see nothing. I was too young and I wanted to become a known figure. "Okay, but remember me," I said. I wanted a permanent place in their hearts; I knew I couldn't live life like this.

"We'll remember you," one said, and I loved that feeling.

I have never believed in God, even as a child the idea seemed too far-fetched. I have never had any drive to follow a religious thought in life. Like many the idea of there being a heaven or hell is a fantasy to me. I was too young to die. What three-year-old kid has ever killed himself? So that was not an option.

The man then said, "Oh no, you have to at least go to a mental hospital. You're going to ruin the whole world."

At that moment I felt, I was better than everyone in the world, and no one could tell me what to do.

I saw the same group of people the following night, and they all looked at me. I looked at the guy who I asked what he was thinking, and he said, "Ali, I'm gay."

"What?" I said, "Then what was all that laughing about gay people?"

Then he said something to me that gave me knowledge that would stick me for the reminder of my life, he said "You're a kid, you're supposed to be out there having fun, not asking these questions."

I used what other people were doing, and what "you're supposed to be doing at that age" to keep me somewhat blended with people, however all the acting was fake. Without it I would have been the first four-year-old homeless person.

Nevertheless, I too thought of the event as pretty shocking, so I went over to my mom who was not too far away, and walked off with her. At that moment I realized that nothing was going to change, and this vicious pattern would repeat over and over again. I kept that event as one of my deepest secrets; I repressed thoughts such as these and subconsciously told myself to keep doing these actions, and I would one day reign. I became stupid, not interpreting reality in a sane way. I could have been happier but I chose the path less followed. I began confusing reality.

I knew I had to do something because where was my life going? Is it ever to go anywhere? When would I feel real? Why am I doing this? My mom had an idea of what went on, and I asked her, "Mom, what am I?"

She had no response but the look in her face told me that she loved me and will always love me. There are other mental patients like me who are vegetable, they do nothing, and feel like nothing, but they are a little happier because of the fact that they don't have to do anything, when in reality anything is better than doing nothing. This to me was insane, why would you want to spend your life like that? They think what they are doing I right because they hurt no one, but in reality people hurt each other in one way or another every day. So, what if I hurt people a little more? I'm experiencing much more than the people that are strapped down, and through more experience one receives more happiness, but I said, "Okay Mom, put me in a mental hospital." I felt as though that was my place in the world, and I was to be analyzed. I knew, however, in the back of my head that I would not stay too long. I wanted the whole world to know about me. I wanted to be the most famous person in the world, as famous as the president.

Chapter 2

I was in Indiana when I was entered into a mental hospital. My mom had checked me in. At first I was talking to some adults about ordinary topics. I found that I could connect with people, and I was ordinary, but it was so boring for me. Life was natural and pretty easy; sure, you had to give some effort but it was normal. Being normal was not enough. I actually made a funny joke to an adult, and he repeated one right back to me. This was what I discovered to be how life is lived, talking about stupid little occurrences that happen all the time throughout life, and making light of it, and in the end it means nothing.

I was about to say some things that were going to enable me never to be happy, things that were illogical and most wouldn't say. I felt it was my purpose to speak nonsense at that moment, because if I didn't I wouldn't be special. As a child I felt I could act up, and I had an alibi, where an adult has none. I could be young and stupid and get away with it. "Why?" I said as I saw people all around me talk, "Why are they talking?" I saw a few laughs, and then I went on. "They're stupid, they're talking about nothing," which is what I thought was true.

So why do people do and say the things they do? Really no reason, they talk and there is never any true meaning in anything anyone says to each other; it is all based on random events that I saw as bullshit. As I write this story now, I know the true meaning of why people like one another and associate events, it either has to do with God, because they are happy, or love. Happiness and the ability to fall in love with someone are the real reasons we are here. God also fulfills spirits to make some people genuinely happy. At that time, I wasn't about to be held down by anything.

I gazed at people talking and thought of the crazy idea that they were all just talking to keep me under control and to try to make me sane. I really hate this thought because it kills me deep inside, knowing that I have no reason. I felt as though nobody's real, and that I have in reason. I felt as though nobody's real, and that is one of the scariest thoughts a human can possibly have. No one was good enough for me. No one, or anything in my life had any meaning. I was deciding my destiny at that moment and I knew I could be a normal human being if I wanted to, but that idea did not last too long. I wanted to make an imprint on the world. Be different. Be unhappy, the worst human to have ever lived. Leave a mark; let it be known that Ali Mazhin lived.

The people simply put me in a confined room. I then delved into myself even more. I had life that I wanted to give off, life that was more human than human. I was able to come up with powerful speech that no man come up with---phrases that not even I could understand. It scared all others and me. I had so much hate bottled up inside me, that every time I thought of myself, I had to let it out or die inside. I did not want to be an average person just living an average life. Every time I talked to someone afterwards, it was staged. Everything I said didn't make sense. I confused others and myself too.

"What am I?" I yelled. I demanded to now, even though I knew nobody could give me an answer that would satisfy me.

"You're crazy," the first person told me, smiling.

"no, I'm not crazy!" I yelled, "You're shit, you're not smart!" I thought I could detect brilliance. The man walked away. "What if I'm not crazy? Everyone is just stupid," I said, yelling out as loud as I can, "Why are all you talking? Who cares! You're all stupid!"

Most laughed, and at the same time had serious looks of fear on their face. I wanted to control life, to temporarily be king. I drained. them of their happiness, and saw them as I saw myself for a brief few moments, miserable with a completely blank look on their faces. They then hated themselves in order to deal with me. I looked at another man, and thought that by the look in his eyes he was smart, "Jesus, look at this guy, he's the best person anyone can be!" A ridiculous statement but I said it. He learned to hate himself so he could understand my thought processes.

One person after the other started coming up to me and told me their thoughts of me. "You're evil," one person said. That kind of scared me as I began to think of myself as being superhuman in a bad way. How could one live with a thought like that? Knowing that every second of your existence is opposed by the devil. It is hell on Earth, and that is how I feel most of the time.

"No, I'm not evil," I told the man.

"You're the most dangerous man in the world," another said.

"Why?" I yelled again with power, and this time I really meant it, why was everyone here? When the question I should have asked was, "Why am I here?" At that moment there was complete silence in the whole floor, and you could say I "Hit them all." They experienced my reality, nothingness. It was like a love so strong that if I died most would kill them. That is how powerful the force of my love was. I felt I was something more than a wild child having fun, something supernatural. I was genuinely insane.

"You're as dumb as a fish" one said.

"You killed the dinosaurs" the next person approached me and said.

Wow, I thought, *am I forever? Have I been here before and controlled past populations in generations of the past?*

"You're savior of the human race," now I knew it, I would be analyzed and be treated and viewed by everyone as someone who is definitely not a normal human.

Now some of the smartest people in the country were flown from all parts of the country to figure out where I was. This was what I wanted. I loved knowing that some of the most brilliant people in the world knew about me, "Ali Mazhin." I thought to myself what "I" thought was. I was nobody in life trying to be someone special. I was somebody who wanted to go out in life as a legend, a mogul in history.

As a child I repressed every label that was given to me, and pretended as though I never heard of the truth. This was the only way I could learn to live with myself, by denial. The truth I always knew, and I tried never to think about it. The world and everything in it was mine. I could have anything I wanted, and had the power to kill anyone I wanted.

In my eyes I saw myself as someone who was trying to find how to talk perfectly with people. I talked as a child with the adults in the institution for a couple of sentences, but then all the confidence that I thought I had died. I built trust in a conversation and destroyed it later; it was my way of murder. I was blank, and I thought anyone who I talked with was like a God. I gave people way too much respect, leaving non for me. All they really had was confidence. At the time, I hated them for having it, because I had none. I hated them so much for having it that I would not even have cared if they had just died in front of me.

At an early age, my self-image was that of a confused young boy. I viewed myself as a dork with low self-esteem. One time, while conversing with a psychologist, out of nowhere came burning in my chest laughter to bring the person who I was talking to down the floor. I felt normal, so normal that life was a big joke. I felt like I had control over anything---even people. I stopped whatever conversation was going on and I fell. It gave rise to a powerful force of hate.

"You can talk and love yourself" is what I vaguely remember saying to one, showering him with a love that no one else could give. They did not know there was such a thing as love to this degree. "Can I such your dick?" I said forcefully. Okay, I'm gay, that's what I'm supposed to do. I had to kill the person. I thought it was the only thing to do.

"No," the psychologist said, hiding behind a bookshelf. I jumped out of my seat as I threw a table over trying to pull his pants down. I would, if given the opportunity then, suck his dick, tell him he's gay, and later call him shit, and happiness would no longer exist. He would never be able to love again; he could now only love me. This person however was strong. He knew me, and saw the insanity in me and viewed it as my problem. The majority of people however are not like this. I thought during the whole process that maybe I was just gay and could not accept it; and if I came out of the closet, I'd be Okay. My purpose with that psychologist was not to make love to him. It was to control him. I wanted his soul. It would have made me feel powerful, and given me some form of life.

So, as though nothing seemed wrong, I tried to act normal at times to show myself that I was not crazy, and have bursts of erratic behavior that I'd forget quickly. I had a chemical imbalance and I thought it made me better than everybody else. For the next 15 or so years, I repeated similar acts with a countless number of people to later become the most powerful man in the world. I became a hostage to the devil.

It was after a couple of more days in the hospital that I started asking more questions about my and other people's existence. "I'm smart," I told someone. I thought I was the smartest man to ever live.

"What?" One man said laughing.

"No, I'm really smart," I said.

"Okay," the man said, "We will administer some standard tests to determine your intelligence." The man sat me in a chair. He was also in a chair across the room from me. "Okay, ready?" he said.

"Yes."

With one hand he dropped a book and at the same time with the other hand he threw a paper airplane.

"Quick, what just happened?" The expression on my face showed it all, a look of confusion. I could not remember what had been dropped. The thoughts that were going through my head were the exact words, "Why would I do that, why is he there, and more clutters of the question, am I doing what is right? Why?" He looked at me with a look of laughter and told me, "Tell yourself you're crazy," then my life would make sense, and the madness would end.

I actually listened to him for a second. *I'm crazy*, I thought. "Nooooo!" I yelled. I could not accept it. At that moment everything made sense to me, I knew if I would tell myself I was crazy, that I would lose all power, get fat, and actually not cause any harm to the world. I then told myself that I'm crazy again, because I would lose what little life that I had. My pretend world of false and illogical thinking would come to an end and the evil joys of my life would fade away. I wanted to live differently.

I was getting more and more stupid by the day; I could not even ask a question or even look at people without having some sort of psychological drama happening. "People are chickens!" I said.

"What are you talking about?" one said.

"Yes, look at them, they are like chickens ruffling their feathers." I meant just like chickens that ruffle their feathers to unwind, people laugh to unwind and it looks similar.

"You're crazy!" I heard, "No I'm a bad-ass."

"What's a bad-ass?" was the response.

"Someone who doesn't care!" I just thought of myself as a bad-ass like Marlin Brando in *The Godfather*.

I wanted to know all the information that at that age I thought was the most important. I talked with a lady, and she told me that in life, you go to school, find a job, buy a house, find someone you love, and be happy. "We like each other" she said.

I thought to myself, that I have to be the best at all of these things. I was now concerned with the best of everything. "What is the best school you can go to?" I asked with aggression.

She said, "I guess Harvard University."

I had a feeling that I would not attend because I felt I was smart in that way. "What about the best school that is somewhat hard to get into with the best reputation?" I asked. I had to know so I could live a fulfilled life.

"Well I guess the University of Southern California."

I knew then that that is where I'd end up. "What jobs make the most money?"

"Doctors, lawyers, business men," she said.

"Wow business men," I said, these people sound like the biggest bad-asses ever. I knew that I was going to study business. "What is the hardest profession to get into? The one that requires the most studying and work to be completed?"

She laughed and named some professions and said, "A plastic surgeon." My father had a big nose, and I knew my nose would grow when I was older.

"I am going to have a nose job, and have sex with my plastic surgeon." She laughed with a sense of love.

I still wanted to know the hardest school subject there was, and at this time I had spoken to hand chosen chemists, physicists, mobsters, doctors, and businessmen. Every science and profession are understandable. It all makes sense. They are all subjects with a bunch of laws that are usually tied in together. Whereas, in Business the possibilities are endless, scientifically, accounting is the most difficult profession, and there are loopholes to everything. Accounting, I learned, was the subject that required the most effort. I would remember that.

"What do you want?" she then asked.

"I want to live in the best place, and make the most money and have the hottest wife," I said. I knew deep down inside that I did not have the power to do any of this, so I had to find someone already with all these toys, and just be with that person for the rest of my life.

I found that people play sports for fun, and watch them for entertainment. "What is the best sport?" I wanted an objective answer, and of course that is impossible.

"It depends on your taste," she said. Of all the sports the easiest to follow, most straight-forward, and simplest I found was basketball.

"Basketball is the best sport in the world!" I said.

"I want to talk to the best basketball player in the world." A kid who I later met in the institution when I reached 19 was shown to me. His facial expression showed, "Why are you doing this?" I looked back and felt the same way. I sucked his dick and felt no joy; I knew what I was doing was wrong.

Magic Johnson and Isaiah Thomas were both flown in and were to speak with me. "So, you guys are the best in the world? Why do you guys play? How does it all work out? You guys are too stupid to handle the business operations of the game!"

They looked at each other and said, "Yeah, you're right, but who cares, we have businessmen who handle all these matters for us."

"No" I said "you're too stupid, you can't connect with those people." I had to know why they were living. A businessman for the sport was present and I told him, "They are too stupid to do business with you, in the future you guys are not going to be able to do business with each other. It is just what's going to happen." Magic and Isaiah were in front of me and I thought, *What is it?* What was I looking for? *Oh, it's just the gay thing.* "Are you guys gay?"

"Yes," they said with an attitude of what is the big deal with being gay.

"If you're gay then suck each other's dicks!"

"Well okay." They did.

"Now fuck each other." They did and I thought to myself that nothing in life means anything, why am I doing this? I can have anything, and I still wouldn't be happy. Life's reality sucks. I'm just one of the few people who want to show the world that idea in an extreme manner.

While still in the institution, I wanted to hear what normal people talked about so I got in groups with people who were trained in how to talk with me, and I flat out could not carry on a conversation; nothing was interesting, it seemed as though nothing was real. Just fake talk.

"Youuuuu can talk and are so bad-ass at doing it, you're the best person in the world at talking in tables." That gave me joy; the most power of my own words had against the flow of the conversation that gave me pleasure. I thrived off of it, it was insanity, and I continued to communicate in a nonsense fashion in as many situations where I could, by trying to have complete control in every situation, and try to (in my eyes) be better than everyone else.

After my remark, the fellow got up, left and said, "I can't do this."

"Why, who cares?" was my remark back to him. I began as a child to focus on the worst-case scenarios of every situation. I brought bright people down and that gave me life. After bringing everyone down in conversation, I would actually feel bad, and quickly make myself feel better by showering deep love. This is how people loved me, and hated me.

But what do normal people talk about without knowing of my presence? A lady took me and tapped into telephone conversations, while I listened. I could not understand what people were talking about, but in every conversation there was a flow. People connected with one another. They were all the same. "Who cares? They are talking about nothing." It was all such bullshit to me. *They are all stupid*, I thought. *I am the only smart person in the world. I am the only person who knows true life.*

"I want to talk to deep thinkers," I said.

"Well, there are philosophers. They think and analyze the world."

"I want to talk to the smartest philosopher in the world."

"We can't so that, he knows you, we already contacted him and he said he would not see you."

"Why not?" I can never be happy, I have to talk to him." And that line, "I can never be happy," got me anything I wanted. People now had to resort to giving me what I wanted. They had no other choice.

A day went by and they said, "Okay we found him, the smartest philosopher in the country"

"I don't believe you. I want the smartest one. How do I know if he's so smart? Has he won awards? Medals?" The people showed me astounding evidence that indeed this was one of the smartest philosophers alive. I saw him; in my eyes he looked like the smartest man I'd ever seen. I thought to myself I was like him, a genius. I thought we were the same, equals. He had a look in his eyes that he understood everything and wasn't fazed by anything. My first line to him was, "Look everyone's stupid, why are they doing this? Why?

He replied with an answer understanding my viewpoint. I said some queer lines that only I and a handful of people can understand, and he gave me both negative, and the positive aspects of my statement. He understood all the energy I was giving off. After 30 seconds of talking to him I went blank, nothingness had arrived. My demons came out. "Jesus look at you, you are the biggest, best bad-ass in the world, and you can get anything you want." I was in love with the guy; he was like a god to me, my ideal person. "What are you thinking?" I said with a grin.

He laughed and told me a philosophy quote. "Who cares!" I said. "Now what are you thinking?" I asked, and I was right, we both knew it I gave negative vibes, but without words to describe them. "Ohhh, I see, in life you just go. Just move and go along. Now what are you thinking?" He basically said he disliked me in words I can't describe.

"Ahhhh," I said. It hurt me, and I yelled, "Who cares!" I was amazed this guy thought of thoughts back to back as quickly as he did and they just keep coming. I can think for a day or so and have a couple quick normal conversations then I go either blank or I'm hurting inside.

"Oh my God" he said "My life no longer has any meaning. Why do you think I didn't want to see you? I have no more reasons to live, who cares?

We connected deeply; we reached the lowest point of existence together, absolute nothingness and a deep hatred for life---basically a nervous breakdown. At that moment we shared the belief that there is no true meaning to existence, and there is no longer reason to go on. He had obviously already known the philosophies or theories of a meaningless life, but he had never had it connected to him on a level that I did.

"I'm going to kill myself," he said.

"No, you are too bad-ass, live and research me your whole life." I said.

"Okay then you kill yourself, that is the only way I will live," he said.

I thought about it and how much I loved this person way too much for him to kill himself; he was basically the best human being in the world I'd met so far, and probably the best I'd ever meet, perfection.

"Okay," I said, "But you are going to research me your whole life."

"I will, I love you," he said.

"You can never stop writing about me." I agreed to everyone to shit myself, and people around me were getting happy that they actually might see me die. A glimpse of joy reached everyone, including myself. Just think, it could all be over and everything would go back to normal. A gun was brought to me. I held it up to my head, with the philosopher by my side, actually almost pulling the trigger and then felt the devil saying, "It's not going to end yet."

I felt as meaningless as life was, it must go on. I was two people in one, a good person and Satan. I was close to pulling the trigger, but I felt as though I had not lived enough life, I had more destroying to do. "Nooo" I yelled, "I'm going to kill myself. Who cares!" A look of disbelief reached everyone. My life was as low and meaningless as one could quite possibly imagine. I could not kill the devil.

The philosopher took the gun from me, was on the same wavelength as I was, laughed and blew his brains out. "Oh no, look at what you have done, he was one of the most special people on the planet," one said. He was in a handful of the most special, and Godly like people that ever existed. I deeply regret what happened. I was on a mission to feel and experience the most painful lows and joyous feelings of the world. I then thought, *I am even better than him, nothing can ever stop me*. He died, I lived. I was a bad person. I wanted to rule the world in some sort of way. "I want to see the president, then I'll be happy," I said next.

If I could learn from a ruler of that magnitude, I would understand the world and be normal. I knew in the back of my mind I'd kill him, too. "No way," they said, "That's one person we are not going to get you to see." I understood; I had a little grasp of reality.

Chapter 3

I was very confused at this point. I had to pinpoint the problem and see what was wrong with me and what I could do to fix the problem. "I want to talk to the toughest person in the world," I said. They searched around all Junior High Schools and one kid from Michigan named Tim was flown in.

I was behind bars and he showed up in front of me. He looked a little sticky and large, and he pointed to himself and said with a smile, "I'm the toughest guy in the world."

I was amazed, he had a strong sense of confidence and nothing would shake him. I was happy to meet him because he was unique. I laughed with him and I burned inside. "I'm gay," he said.

"No way, you're too bad-ass." I wouldn't believe a gay person to be tough.

"I love you," he said. There was nothing more to say, he loved me in a way that can't be explained. It's a sort of love where we didn't ever have to see each other again and it would be fine. I had got to him; in a way I made my imprint.

What is next? I thought. I was on a roll, killing everyone; I had to move on.

"I want to talk to the funniest man in the world." I thought talking to a funny man would clear my head and I would see that there is no reason to be depressed. He came and made a few jokes, and I laughed for a little bit, but I was still missing something. I began to bring myself down with negative thoughts. I couldn't bring him down because he was so unhappy. Genuinely happy, something most humans never achieve. He talked for a little while, but there was nothing else to say to him so he left.

"Okay, confidence is what I need. I need to speak to a confident person," so I could see how important of a value confidence is. "I need to talk to the most confident guy in the world." From the Middle East, he was flown in. He kept saying things to me that I couldn't understand, and he wasn't shaken. He kept rambling on happy words. I could not break him. He just laughed at my life and me, "What are you thinking?" I said.

"I just feel bad that you're never going to be happy," he said.

"Never," I said with authority, as if it's something to be proud of.

"Okay, there is no one else for me to see," because it didn't work out. So, I felt I might as well have fun with my life. "I want everyone who wants to see me to come in and talk to me if they want to."

"Okay" they said.

A person was face to face with me who I had met some time in the past. "You're the best person ever I would say," I said.

He laughed and I connected with him. He then flat-out said, "Come on Ali, tell me to kill myself," with a gun in his hand. He saw me and knew what a joke life was.

"No, you're too bad-ass, just go out and make money. You're going to make sooo much money. Just do it, it's the most important thing."

He laughed and said, "Okay, I'll do it for you." He left and I felt fine.

Another person came and said, "Ali please let me kill myself."

"Kill yourself, who cares," I said. We both shared a laugh, and he shot himself in the face right in front of me. It was a mess, blood all over the place. Complete silence and a deep feeling of pain entered my soul.

"I don't know how you can live with yourself," a lady told me. I knew she was right.

Okay it must be sex that I'm missing. "I just want to have sex all day!" I said.

"Sex is something you do if you love someone," a lady said.

"No, I want to have sex all day and I can't feel bad." Later there were about ten girls in the span of two days that I had sex with (of course I had no feeling). One after the other had sex. Each girl was different so I experienced many personalities. There were a few girls that I did like, and that liked me back, but I was not ready to settle down. Some were boring and monotonous, and some I really liked. "I want to be with you forever," I said to a girl giggling with her, I've finally found my soul mate.

"Okay" she said. I felt as though I had a companion, and it was natural.

Whoa, I thought, *it's all over*, *I've found true love and I can be with this girl* and she would also love me. "I'm happy," I said.

"Finally," they thought, "We made him happy." I then thought of how I made it a point to be happy, so I let her go. Then when I was alone for a second I died inside. Girl or guy, any time I tried to love, it seemed too thought of a task, I was too weak to stand up on my two feet. I felt so empty inside.

Another girl came and I just made eye contact and that was enough for her to say, "I can't do this," referring to having sex with me. She felt the negative energy I was giving off. I felt evil.

I was just getting started on my rampage. I wanted to see what the entire world had to offer. "I want to be treated like a king." I said.

"Okay," one said. I was seated in a chair, with three women surrounding me. One was fanning me, one was feeding me grapes, and the other just stood there rubbing me. The three girls were all smiling too. I was just sitting there thinking of nothing, but feeling so powerful. I knew it was all staged so it didn't mean anything to me. I was happy for a second, and then told them, "You're shit." Or in other words, "Get away from me." Even the life of a king could not satisfy me.

Psychology was where all my problems arrived. So, if I learned about it I could help myself. “I want to talk the smartest psychologist in the world or else I can never be happy.” A search was underway and they found someone at the top of their class at Cornell. He was one of the brightest people in the world. He was pulled out of school to talk to me. I was out face to face with him.

It was a dark night and the first thing he said in agony was, “I hate myself.” He said it with deep pain. I tried to laugh about it but I couldn’t. I was also in deep pain. I felt as though there was a force crushing me to the ground, telling me to kill myself, but I knew it was too great of a task. The same energy was given off from me to him. “I hate myself,” he said again. I was not having fun with this guy. I thought to ask to suck his dick, but why? It would be ridiculous; I couldn’t hide behind the fantasy gay craze anymore.

“You are here for a reason,” he said excruciatingly. I was excited when he said this because no one else had ever told me anything like this. “To control the population.” I couldn’t take it, I wanted to walk away, but I had to say something. From an earlier conversation with someone I knew I would end up at U.S.C. someday, “You’re going to make so much money and you’re going to teach at U.S.C.” I wanted him to become one of my teachers. He listened, I walked away, and another life was now about to be lived for me. The world was mine.

“You’re evil” one of the personnel said. That is what I was now labeled. There are a countless number of people who think they are evil, but are really normal. From these, only about 30,000 in the world can be thought of as being “bad seeds.” These are the wrong doers who stand out from the average psycho. All these people create their torment and cause rampage due to it. Most can be treated and are in need of some definite help. I was one of them.

“Okay,” I thought I needed to talk to someone who is evil. I began to think there is such a thing as an evil person. In reality however, I do not believe in pure evil, because it is just too far-fetched. Everyone can be happy. “I want to talk to someone who is evil,” I said. After a couple of days, they said they had found someone who was evil. I was flown to India. The person spoke English; his name was Habib, in his 20s, from a small town in India.

It was dark when I finally met him face to face. The first thing I said was, “So, you are evil?”

"Yes," he said.

"How many of us are there?"

"There are many of us."

"Wow," I thought, "I am like other people, but these people keep being evil secret. I am part of a clan that is set to ruin the world. I have a purpose. I am a part of a handful of supernatural humans, and I am just one of the dumb ones who does not know his purpose. All other evil people know they were put on Earth for the reason of destruction. I did not know what else to say to Habib. I thought that was all there was to it, my life's purpose was to commit wrong doings. I had it all figured out. I was just going to live the rest of my life without worry. He had a very straight face when I talked to him. The message that he wanted to send was for me to realize that I was this kind of person, and for humanity's sake, not to act upon it, like others would do.

Okay, I felt, *I'm evil*. I still could not find a constant state of well-being with myself. I started to walk away slowly as if this person was real. "Youuuu can… (something where you think of words that describe feeling your body)" I yelled, he stood still, like a mogul. "Youuuu can… (another body part)! Again, he stood still and straight-faced, with a look of the reality of mine---nothingness, no laughter or good thoughts. "Youuuuu can… (it became ridiculous)!" I said as I was walking away ready to leave.

"Haaa, haaa, haaa," he cracked, he could not hold himself back.

I ran back towards him with joy, and said, "Jeese you are sooo bad-ass." His hysterical laughter came across immensely. You could tell the man had never laughed so hard with so much joy.

"I have been trained for three years to know how to deal with you," he said. I was amazed. This guy was special.

"What are you?" I asked. "I am the smartest person in India. I have taken a countless number of tests, and completed with thousands of people to have a discussion with you."

"Haa, haa" I laughed. He laughed hysterically. "Can I suck your dick?" He nodded yes with laughter. I saw an amazing person while I was doing it. He was real. I saw his face show off all of his true personality. He was a unique and exceptional human being. I imagined what it would be like to be him. "You're gay!" I said.

"Haa, haa, haa," he laughed He was obviously not gay. We were both experiencing bliss.

"You're shit," I had to say it, I thought that of everyone. He was still in laughter. I had never seen anyone like this person. He was godlike. A person with his own mind, idiosyncratic. I usually would then flee the situation, running as if I had taken his heart and soul, and forget about him. But not this person, he was the most special person I had ever come across. I still think that today too.

As I came down off my high, I realized what I had done to the person, and it was painful. I would usually flee the scene and pretend as though the whole incident had never happened, but I did not flee. This was the only person to this day that I ever stayed with to talk to after my act of killing. I started to cry. His face was in peace as this happened and he was till in a good mood.

"Jesus look at you" I said. "You never ask yourself the question, why? You never doubt yourself."

"I know" he said joyously, as if he was being treated as a God.

"So, what do you think about then? How can you never ask yourself why something is happening? How do you just talk to people?"

He responded by telling me how when you talk to people you automatically have curiosity as to what they are thinking, compassion. Never starting with only negative thoughts towards the person. "It's all good, life is meant to be enjoyed and to be with people," is what I think he was trying to say.

"You never ask yourself why?"

"No, it never comes in my mind."

"What are you thinking?" I said.

"I am thinking of four different things at the same time." All the thoughts he was thinking were natural happy thoughts. Nothing meant anything. Some thoughts of course mean nothing to another person, and some meant acts of positive feeling towards the other person. I learned what the basis of being happy was, positivism and compassion. I was grounded; this guy demonstrated how all my thoughts about life and reality were garbage.

"You're like a god," I told him. "You're going to build a church. You're going to Harvard business school and you're going to study accounting. You're going to make so much money!" He stood there listening to the path I was setting for his life. He absorbed all of my comments and was now destined to follow my words. "What if I never met you?" I said. "What would you become?"

"I would have been happy," he said, as if he didn't care because of how much he loved me.

"But what about Survival of the Fittest, it's not true." I cried. I refused to believe in this theory because I wasn't fit.

"It is true, I'm fit."

I disbelieved the theory because I thought that with the theory there was no way of a God existing. How could we all be equal when some people outlast each other in life due to the intelligence? If we are all meant to be happy, then how are some people meant to last in this world, and some people die? Shouldn't God give us all the same odds of surviving? If God loves us all then why can't some people last in this world? I repeated how the theory was a crock of shit.

I felt as though I would die for Habib. So, I told him, "You're going to teach Accounting at U.S.C., and I will later kill myself for you." That is how I eventually wanted it to end, die for the best. "Survival of the Fittest, tell me it's not true, so I can be happy." I meant this statement to be said while he was teaching me at U.S.C.

"Okay," he said. This was the destiny I created for myself. This is how it was going to end; I'd die for the one I loved the most. Habib was still happy, and he took me to his brothers, "Look at this guy!" he said showing me off to his three brothers.

"Jesus, you're brothers! They're just as bad-ass as you!" They all laughed. I got to each of them. "You guys are going to look for the cure to AIDS. You're never going to find it," I said, "never!" At the time I thought I had the disease and was infecting everyone.

I feel as if I'm one half good, and one half bad.

Schizophrenia is what I am writing about folks, but it is all a game and I know I am really normal inside. I speak a strange language. Often people with a personality disorder refer to themselves as, "We or Us" instead of, "Me or I," as if they are more than one person. Everyone in life likes to think of him or herself as special. I wanted to think of myself as better than God.

I wanted the best, so I said, "I want to be with the smartest people in the world." A group of 7 or 8 people was gathered, and I started blabbering away queer talk. "You guys understand me?" I said.

"Yes" they nodded.

I looked around and asked, "Who is this guy?"

"I'm Frank, I'm the smartest man in the world." I said something crazy, and he understood me from all angles, thinking four things at the same time.

"You're going to be the president of U.S.C., you'll be president when I'm there, you're going to go to Harvard." I looked at the group, and said, "Let's all be together forever." I could have had that happen. I could have lived with a group of masterminds, it sounded ideal. But I lost motivation quickly; because I did not know what I wanted.

I moved on after that incident, and wanted to do it all over again, because there's nothing else to do. *Maybe I'm crazy*, I thought. "I want to talk to somebody that's crazy." I said. They took me to another mental institution and all the way to a chamber in the bottom, where all the true crazies were. I saw someone behind bars, seated in a chair, and in a straight jacket.

"He's crazy," my escort said. I still didn't think to talk to him.

"So, you're crazy?" ---no response. I could tell he was thinking something but I didn't know what. I thought him and me as close alike as I can get said. I was asking to be together with him forever. I would find a companion like me and be happy. Someone I could relate to. He gave no response, "Oh, we are so alike that there is no reason for us to be together, we're the same, life would be boring, we should go our separate ways." Again, no response. Deep down inside I knew I was not like him, because I could not talk, and be comfortable with himself, while my eyes would be wandering all around, at the same time saying stupid comments. I left.

"We found someone like you," a person said.

They showed me someone else in a different institution and my first words were, "You have sex with people and call them shit?"

"Yeah, but I don't want to ruin the world with my condition," he said. I laughed and thought to myself *maybe I should stay in an institution forever. He is right.*

I looked at the personnel and they said, "Say the word 'yes,' and we will never let you out of the institution." If I said yes there would be no way out, they would use every barrier possible and with all my power it would be impossible to leave. It would be legal if I had said yes to the barriers forever.

I made a statement to the inmate that basically came out as, "I don't like myself."

He said, “You don’t like yourself?” as if to say how in the world can you live not liking yourself? A look of disbelief is what he gave me.

I looked straight at the personnel and I knew I didn’t want to be committed like he was, “Noooo!” I yelled I didn’t want to be in an institution forever. And that was the end of that. I knew I was like no one.

“I want to talk to the smartest woman in the world, and then I’ll be happy” I asked. An older woman probably 40 years old greeted me. By the way she looked I could tell she was brilliant, so bright, and real. I used all of my insane talk to try to outsmart her. I just kept saying one thing after another that I didn’t even know what I meant. I tried to control her, but I couldn’t. Everything she would say back to me put me in place. I felt like a confused young boy. I tried so hard to keep up with her mentally, that finally the message same through to me, *Why am I here?* That was what it all came down to. I was yelling the word, “No,” in my head with disbelief. She mentally beat me. I was in love.

However, as a kid the only thing I could do was repress the idea that I was there for no reason. It was over, I met my match, “You and me are going to get married, no one will ever love you as much as I do. If only I were older so that we can fuck!” I was serious and she only smiled. “All we are going to do when we get married is have sex! That all we are going to do, call me when I’m older and we will be together.” When I said, “Call me when I’m older and we will be together,” I had started to formulate an idea of how my life path will go, what various stages I will go through, and when I’ll stop living a lie and become an adult. I was going to start living sane by the time I was 19 years old. I could no longer be stupid after that age, because then I’d really be crazy.

“You’re going to teach at U.S.C.” This school obsessed me. It was to be, “my” school. She was to be one of my professors. My goal was to see as many examples of the best-fit people in the Survival of the Fittest theory.

By now the experts wanted to put me as far away from the people as possible. “Go inside the prison cell,” they tried to tell me.

“No,” I said. I thought I was too bad-ass, better than them all. I did not want to be locked up, and what could they do, they could not mentally force me to do anything. I was stronger. A person made some small talk with me, he told me to look at something, and as I turned around I was pushed into a cell, and they locked it shut. I laughed, "How did they do that?"

"We planned it," one said. They had put me in the deepest chamber in the institution, so I would have as little contact with people as possible. They wanted to seclude me from everyone so I would not "hit" anyone else. "We put a gun on the table," one said. I laughed; they had tricked me into the cell. A few days passed. "Kill yourself, you're crazy," one said.

"No. I'm a bad-ass! I don't care!"

"Okay we secretly videotaped you in the cell yesterday." The tape was shown to me. The taped showed me laughing to myself.

"Ahh Ahh Ahh," I laughed standing straight up for hours just giggling to myself. I was laughing at the damage that I had done to the world. After a while of standing around I thought to myself, *Okay, I might as well kill myself, this is ridiculous, what am I?* That is as far as the thought went. I could not even come within 2 feet of the gun they placed beside me. My body would just not allow it. It was physically impossible. I found myself alone. All that was given to me was food, and a restroom. Maybe the experts thought by not talking to me that I could no longer cause harm. After all this technique does make sense. However, I started to feel restless, my body needed to have interaction.

It got so bad that I started to scream with no one around, "Ahhhhhhhh!!!!" I pulled my hair in agony. The Earth started to shake and the room started to move. I can't do this at will, but sometimes it happens when I get to my lowest point. The few people listening to my sounds from above heard me and came down to try to calm me down. It helped; I need people, just as everyone does. I figured not only do I have no place on this Earth; I have no place by myself. I should do the noble thing and just die. "Kill me." I said, "I can't do it myself so kill me, I want the best assassin to come and kill me face to face."

Hand chosen, one was flown in. Face to face with the man, "So you're the best assassin?" I said as he pointed the gun to my chest. "You might as well kill me," I said, he had a serious face on with no reaction to what I said. If I had shut up for one minute I probably would have been dead. "No don't kill me." I said. He waited around, "I guess you have to kill me," I said while mumbling some other words, he stood there for five more minutes with the gun pointed at me and walked away. He couldn't do it. We both knew I should have been dead but some force stopped that from happening.

"Okay" I said to the personnel later. "You have to kill me without me knowing you're there." That's how I thought would be the only way I could die. One sharpshooter after another hid behind walls and found crevices where their bullets could hit me. Silence is all I heard, until the tiniest peep of sound came; the shooter was ready to fire. "I see you" is what I said. No noise, no shot. Another tried, "I know you're there." I said, while telling myself I didn't want to be killed. It was the only thing on my mind and I had to say the words. "I hate you," is what I heard someone say in anger and frustration. I was the smartest person in the world for I could not be killed.

Chapter 4

"Ahhh let me out!" I screamed in agony. I could not handle being locked up anymore; I thought I could just be normal if they let me out.

"No way, we are definitely never going to let you out."

"Why not!" I said.

"Because the authority of the institution won't let you." I thought no one could beat me, and I could get anything I wanted.

"Who is the person with this authority? Let me talk with the person." He was an authority figure in personnel. "Let me out" I said.

"No, we are going to keep you in," "Youuu… (Something he had thought to himself that meant nothing)." I said "you…" because I could not think these things.

"Ah, ah, ah," he laughed.

"You're the best guard in the world! Let me out,"

"No," he said.

"Who is your supervisor, who is above you?" I demanded to speak with his authority, and it was a senator. I spoke to him first-hand, he was just like everyone else, a normal happy person. It was a ridiculous conversation on my part and I got him to love me and he said he could no let me out. “Who is your authority?” I asked the senator.

The head of the whole state’s Institutional Facility was the last authority. “Let me talk to him!” I demanded. I hate myself,” the head said. I tried the usual love talk and he wouldn’t give in, he repeated, I hate myself.” He wouldn’t say anything else. The conversation was easy to follow because he hated himself to the degree I hated myself, so we talked a normal conversation in my eyes. That is what I have to do to find a friend. He was at home with his family in complete misery, trying to use all of his mental ability to save the world and not let me out. I kept trying to get him to give in, but he wouldn’t give. With pain and agony, one more time he said, “I hate myself.” I knew there was only one way to get out, as bad as I felt about it I had to do it.

I was at the tip of my tongue the whole time and finally felt I had to say it to get my way, “Kill yourself.” Three seconds later I heard a gun fire and he was dead.

“Okay, we’ll let you out, but why are you doing this?” a lady said.

I had to think of a reason, “I deserve a chance to live. Who are you to tell me I can’t live?” I was right, who are they to tell me not to live my life. There was no choice left but to let me free. I was out of the institution, and back with my parents.

My childhood is a blur, but I recall committing many acts of evil. The thought of being inherently evil is the scariest thought I have. Whoever put us here has left us with the choice of being good or bad. People create their own hell; I was addicted to making mine as much of a hell as possible. Good comes as easy to most people, and at birth people choose to be happy. Of course, not everyone is happy, some people have mental illness, making it a tougher task. Their life is more difficult to control than the common person’s is—it’s not fair but that’s life. Some people are breadwinners by nature. From early on I chose to live a negative life. What a bad decision that was. Reform is a tough task and change does not come easily.

I forget easily, and quickly forgot I had even been in an institution, but I was still who I am. “Ali, water the plants,” my mother says.

“Why!” I said hysterically.

"Ali, water the plants," again.

"Why!" I was becoming slothful by nature, never doing anything myself.

"Ali, clean your room," my father said.

"Why?" My parents would always love me no matter what I did.

I was talking to friends of my family about whom I was, and I thought that with all the confusion I was going through that I must be gay and I needed to talk to a gay person. So, I asked, "Can you guys help me find a person to talk to so I can see if I'm gay? Not just someone who says they're gay, but a flamboyant homosexual who truly believes he's gay." My friends laughed and I was kind of embarrassed, but a week or so passed by and they found a friend of a friend's kid who was gay. This person and I met and we talked face to face. "So, you're gay?" I asked.

"Yes," he smiled.

"How do you know if you're gay?" I asked.

"You just know," he replied.

"So, all you are in life is gay, there's nothing else, every thought involves a man?" I asked.

"Yes, it's no big deal."

"You're beautiful." I said to him.

"You're beautiful," he said back.

I felt as though I had reason. "Can I suck your dick?"

"Okay, but I've never done this before."

I did, and I felt real and normal. "You're gay!" I said, he laughed his head back. "You're shit," I said. I stopped.

"You're not gay," he said.

"Then what am I?"

"You're crazy."

"No, I'm not crazy I'm smart. I'm a really smart faggot."

"You're not smart."

"Yes I am. I'm smarter than you, I can defend myself, go ahead try me," I persuaded.

"Okay gays are immoral. What do you say to that?"

I couldn't think of anything. He asked another question and I couldn't come up with a strong comeback. "You're weak," he said.

"No, I'm just gay. I haven't figured it out yet."

"You're crazy." I listened and we both stood there facing the truth.

"So, what now?" I asked.
"Kill yourself."
"No, I can't, I'll always remember this though."
"I will also always remember this."
"So, what about your life?" I asked.
"I can never be happy," he said.
"Who cares?" I said.
"You're funny," he replied.
"Yeah, but I want to be smart." I said.
"You can never be smart. I'm smart and I'll always have that advantage. But I am not funny, I wish I could be funny." We parted touching each other's lives in ways no one could imagine at such an early age. This is my life.

I became bored with life quickly and needed excitement. I would once again start my wild ways. I tried to control everyone by trying to pull all the strings. Children my age from all over the nation were given multiple tests in personality and intelligence, in order to see if they could save lives, and interact with me. There were rarely "average" people that I met at preschool, and first grade. The smartest teachers from all over the country were trained to teach a class with me in it.

I had one teacher who was 60 or so and chubby. He was a very warmhearted person, good by nature. "People sometimes get tired of everyday happenings in life," my teacher said to the class. I felt the teacher was talking only to me.

I approached him and said, "You were talking to me when you said that." He paused and did not know what to say, because he really didn't think anything of his statement.

"Yeah, I guess" he said.

"Can I suck you dick?" I said while the class was just getting out for lunch.

"If you want to."

I did, "You're gay!" I said. A true laugh from his heart was given. I was high, everyone was watching with a look of nothingness. "You're shit," I said and I left him and casually walked away as though nothing happened, feeling like an ordinary kid. During the sex however I would feel insane, on cloud nine, and I knew this was not right, but this is what I needed to do to feel my age. I needed to do these insane things every once in a while when I started to feel different from others to make me once again feel normal. The students in the class would just give a glance of wonder, and would forget about it going back to their normal lives, but where was mine?

I was a shy kid, never saying much to the public. When I sat with my classmates, conversations come about. That's what people do; they talk to each other. I tried to use all my brains and talk with my classmates. It was a challenge each time. One day I was seated next to three girls. The instructor finished talking, I listened and understood him and we were free to talk with each other. I couldn't find any thoughts in my head. I just sat there like a zombie. I could only go with the flow of things that are set to do, never enjoying my life.

"Who are you?" one of the three girls said as they all laughed. They were tired of games and really wanted to talk to me. I just looked at them and laughed that they were correct.

Oh shit, I thought, *they found me out*. I had to rationalize somehow that I was not crazy. *Oh, I'm gay, gay people can't talk to girls*. I thought. *They are the worst people*. I thought. In reality, however, everybody is somebody. There are always traits in a person that describe who they are. "Who are you?" I asked them back.

"We are some of the smartest people in the world, we had to take several tests just to be here!" They laughed and went about conversing with each other. I did feel better because I felt important

As a kid I went to the usual social events. One I remember clearly was in San Francisco. It was a Metallica. This was before their first album came out. They were not big yet. I was in the back of the crowd with a few friends. They were friends of my family. Everyone was doing something; some were moshing, some wavering their hands, some banging their heads, and some ding nothing, but it was still natural to them. I can't even do nothing and feel natural. I stood still, and felt crazy for doing so; I wanted to be like everyone else raising his or her fists in the air, and head banging. *I can do the same*, I thought, I just had to try. *I'm the same as everyone else*, I thought, but wasn't giving effort.

Now, I thought, now was the time to give effort. I started to shake my head back-to-back, awkwardly, I started to yell, "Yeahh." It didn't feel natural. Everyone around me looked at me as if I were an alien. I felt like the worst person to ever live. But I wasn't going to leave the show feeling like that. “Youuu can dance!” I said to an Italian person who I later found out was named Don.

“What?”

“You’re the best natural dancer!” I said.

“I love this guy!” he said with joy turning to his friends.

“Can I suck your dick?” I asked. I did and called him gay, and then shit. He didn’t care though, he liked me. I did the same act to someone I later found out was my brother, who I told, “This guy. Look at this guy, you’re going to make sooo much money. You’re going to be a lawyer.” The two brothers were only a couple of years older than I was at the time. I looked around and found two other confident people. “This guy, this guy is the best 80s person in the world.” I knew the feel of the 80s referring to music and lifestyle.

“I love you.” He responded.

“You’re shit!”

“Oh man,” he said.

I then thought I was the best person in the concert hall. My mood changed from blue to a heightened state of bliss and control, control over every single thing in the atmosphere. The band saw what was going on and began to sing a cover version of a song that was already out, “Am I Evil.” The whole audience was focused towards me, and I became a legend. The song was later put on their first record called, “Kill ‘em All.” Metallica named their third album after me, “Master of Puppets.” The album covers they chose showed two hands on the top of the picture, with many strings, all attached to tombstones. The lyric in the title song, “Master of Puppets” all refer to me.

Many people who I’ve met in childhood wanted a chance to live near me to be closer. They and new people who have never met me went through various tests given by the Experts to have a chance to live near me. I however had no clue, the Experts made sure I didn’t, because I’d go crazy knowing that’s true.

I made various close friends in school, most of which were very special people. One Asian kid named John was my best friend for a while. He was very bright and genuinely happy, and was fit by the Survival of the Fittest theory. One day playing handball, I was standing alone waiting for something to do. “Ali, come on join playing!” he said.

“Yeah!” I instantly loved him.

"Ali did you play handball today?" he asked.

"I played on the swings and in the sandbox." I was so excited someone cared for what I was doing. Walking with him, I felt bonded, but the only thing I could think of was love. This is all I am. I can't hold a conversation with someone if it's not about love. Most people are baffled when they first talk to me because they are drawn into the love that I speak. Most people are never aware of the deep love that is within all of us. This love is my reality. The world would be such a better place if love were on everyone's basis of reality, but it's not. When I meet someone it's as if I'm in love with him or her and I want to hold a special place in his or her heart. I dislike this because people are usually cold, and they want distance. This creates negative vibes, which leads to suffering. However, there are some people who think nothing of this love and proceed in their own thought process. This creates peace and there is no judgmental behavior.

John was one of these good people; our friendship seemed like a project to me because I believed the love we had was gay. I felt uncomfortable and thought of the love as something impure. However, now that I look back I see that love is the basis of happiness and I rejected it, which created personal suffering. I could not accept that I could only love someone. I viewed the love as being gay, and to me it was the worst thing. The last thing in the world I wanted to be was gay.

There are different types of love. I loved John but sexually I was not attracted. This is where love can even get deeper. Without sexual acts, the love you have for someone can get out of control. I do not know how to love someone with sexual desire. I had a gay friend who John knew about. His name was Alfred. "Alfred is gay," I said with haste; this was the reason he did not want to play with us. John knew that Alfred was gay and this was no big deal to him, but he had a smile on his face that indicated that it is not good to be gay. This to me was the most important thing. I had to be perfect and I didn't want someone to laugh at me—that would mean that he or she was better than me.

I viewed gay people as scared and weak. Most gays were an easy target to shove my burden off to. I however, was not like them, nor was I like straight people. There was so much confusion in my head that I didn't know what to do five seconds from any moment. Being so confused about how to live my life right, I lived in ignorance for many more years to come, by denying who I was. People all throughout my life made fun of gay people. The thing, however, is that they don't care. One could really care less. It could sound mean, but it's really not.

With the ability to love also came the ability to hate. I could hate like no one else could. The darkness in my thoughts scared everyone. I overheard some girls talk about some being gay; they laughed. What I got out of it was that people hate gay people. Trying to be normal, I threw my two-sense in, "Yeah, Alfred is the worst person." Silence. I just gave out hate when all others were happy. No one really cares about anything. I giggled to myself. I wanted to be different.

I had a close friendship with Alfred. He was an ugly Hispanic kid my age. He was an outcast and nobody really liked him. We played and had fin like normal kids that age. I sometimes did not ask the questions, what was I? What does the future hold? Where do I fit in? Because the fun we had cancelled it out. It was a mix between everything, which enabled me from having a grip on reality. The psychology I was using was the worst possible, by choice. Why would anyone choose this reality? Because I wanted to be special.

All of my conversations with Alfred were me asking him questions about life that are never asked that often by a young kid. I look back today and I can't believe how stupid I was. "Alfred," I said, "Are you gay?" I asked it because it was the only thing I really cared about the person. This is not a good way to be talking to a friend, but I did not know any better. He nodded his head yes. He was one of the few people who would say yes to this question at a young age. "How do you know if you're gay?" I asked.

"It's just something I know."

I then thought the question, *What is it that's enabling me from being normal?* "It" means that I was gay. "Ohh so you just figured out being gay faster than I did. You're a smart faggot."

"We're not faggots," he said laughing.

"Yes, we're the worst people in the world."

"What's so bad about it?" he asked.

"Sucking a dick, that's disgusting, everything else is okay."

"It's no big deal" he said.

"What about kids?" I asked.

"We're not perfect."

"Why don't you just marry a girl and have kids, girls are the best things in the world?"

"I wouldn't be happy. I don't like girls." He said.

"But if you can get married then just do it," I said. At this time, I felt it was my life's purpose to marry a beautiful girl and be rich, only then would I be happy. *Oh no* I asked myself, I might as well be happy right now. "Can I suck your dick?" I asked without true desire.

"No, I don't love you."

I wanted power. I wanted to rule him. I felt bad.

"You're beautiful," I told him.

"You're beautiful," he told me back.

I said some stupid remark that he said nothing to, "Why don't you answer me?"

"Because you think you're special, you're not special."

"Oh, so I'm supposed to just sit here like a faggot then?" I hated moments with no talking. I felt that there was no energy, but my energy was in all the wrong places. "What are you thinking?" I asked.

"Is my mom going to make dinner tonight!" he said with disbelief.

"Geese, you're so bad-ass, how can you think like that?" I asked.

"You don't even get that!" he said laughing.

In other conversations with Alfred, I told him how I felt, that I was the worst person, and I asked him to try to feel the same way, and to try to duplicate my thought process. The next day, he tells me, "I tried for an hour of how you think, and I hated it. I felt like a zombie, and hated everything. I felt no enjoyment. The future was depressing. My dad said something to me that I didn't respond. How can you live like that?"

"Yeah, that's what it's like all the time!" I said.

"How can you live with yourself? Why don't you like yourself?" he said.

"Come here you faggot, let me suck your dick." I yelled with joy.

"No, I hate you." I had no reaction. "You're not gay," he said.

"How did you know?" I said.

"You're crazy, and you're going to ruin the whole world. Kill yourself."

"No, I'm going to kill myself" I responded. All of this talk made me think during the next few days. *I have to get my act together, something has to change* or else my behavior would be like this forever. I knew I could stop the madness if I wanted to, but all the fun would die out. All I had to do was listen to the thoughts in my head telling me that what I was doing was insane, but I was still a kid and I should be having fun. Later I put my mood in a very serious manner. I became very "Real." I was trying to change and become normal.

The next time I saw Alfred, I would not even talk to him. He noticed quickly. "You don't like me anymore, why don't you like me?" he said.

"Sorry, Alfred, I have to do this; just know that you're the best one." I felt the ability to be normal was within me, and it would take a lot of time to find myself. Alfred did not know what I was talking about. Deep down inside I wanted to kill him and I was destroying myself at the same time. I wanted him to feel as I felt. We stopped hanging out. I would continue this roller coaster of confusion for years to come.

There was an 18 – year – old babysitter who sometimes listened to Alfred and I conversing. She drove us to various places; she was sort of a loser but very kind. I was telling Alfred I was gay and she said, "No, you're not gay." I was so happy she said that.

"Yeah, gays are the worst people." I said looking at Alfred. "You and me are perfect for each other," I said to her; I was about five at the time. "If only you were older, I'd go out with you."

She said back to me, "Yeah and all we'd do is have sex."

I wanted a wife at the age of five. I had to make a move to guarantee such a position. "Let me touch your tits."

"No," she said laughing. The idea was ridiculous to her.

"Okay, I'm just going to say whatever is on my mind all the time from now on." I wanted to find out who I was, so anything that popped in my mind I would say. The two were silenced. "Tell me who I am," I said in both powerful and confused way. I wanted to be better than the both of them, when in reality this is an insane viewpoint.

"You are a very confident person," she said. At the time, even if I were told I was confident, it would not change my viewpoint of myself. On the outside I wanted to look like a God, indestructible and untouchable, but inside I was as fragile as an infant. "You are very good looking, you will be very handsome when you are older," she said.

"I want to touch your tits," was the first thing that came to my mind. She laughed at what I had said. The next thing that popped in my head was something a queer would say. As I made the statement Alfred looked back and forth in the car to see whom I was talking to. He thought I was talking to him, when I was conversing with her. This kind of situation now happens all the time in my life. I have experienced it for myself also, when a friend says something to another friend face to face, the comments would just fly over the friend to the third person who was not in the conversation. The third person, the person I was really aiming the statement at, understands the statement but is bewildered that it turned out like that. The friend who I talked to acts as if nothing important was said, and brushes off the statement. The third person starts looking all over the place to see whom I was talking to.

In the car ride I said, "Look Alfred, I can talk to girls."

"Yeah, but its fake." Today I agree it was fake, however I had the confidence of a fish so nothing came out right.

"Geese you're a tough fruitcake. Can I suck your dick?" He was sick of my shit and gave up. "Okay, I'll let you suck it!"

"No, don't do it Ali, you're not gay," the babysitter said.

"Yeah, I'm not a faggot like Alfred, just let him live his life sucking cock. Let me fuck you." I said referring to her.

The driver then said, "You're too young, wait until you're 18, and then we'll have sex."

"Okay when I turn 18, you're going to find me wherever I am and we are going to get married. No one will ever love you as much as I do."

She believed everything I said, "Okay, but you have to promise me you will still be friends with Alfred."

"Okay," I said, but I knew our friendship would not last that long, he wasn't special enough. "Just let me touch your tits." I said.

"No!" it just wasn't right.

"Tell me who I am."

"You're a strong, charming, funny, interesting person," she said.

"You love me," I said. "You can never find another man in this life to love as much as you love me."

She laughed and knew it was true. I was testing the boundaries of love to the fullest degree. Love should never have to be toyed with. It is one of the beautiful gifts that God gave us.

In her house later, while Alfred was asleep, she pulled me to her room and said, "Ali I'll let you touch my tits, I don't want you to turn out gay." She pulled her blouse up with her tits hanging down and she looked at me. I touched away with a big smile on my face. *Wow this is the most fun I've ever had*, I thought, *what a beautiful thing girls are*. I had a genuine feeling of confidence and I was having fun. I wanted the moment to last forever, but I knew there was another level to love.

"Let me fuck you!" I said convincingly.

"No!" she said.

"Why not!" I said with ignorance, she stood there and could not think of a reason not for me to fuck her. She loved me and I loved her. She was kind of lonely too, because no one had ever paid so much attention.

"Okay but you're the only one, don't tell anyone anything." She pulled down her pants and I was on top of her. I started intercourse unprotected. The feeling came again: Bliss, pure happiness, and insanity. I was high. I felt that no other human could achieve this feeling. It took me a long time to get to the point where I had gotten.

"You're gay!" I said. I couldn't even say what gay meant. Me saying the other person was gay, girl or guy, was just a statement explaining that I thought the other person was like me. By common definitions, it was crazy. We were both experiencing bliss. There was a bond that is virtually impossible for two people to achieve.

"I love you," she said. Here it came again, who I was, and what I had to do to everyone.

"You're shit!"

"No, why do you say that?" she said. I laughed pulled out and walked away as if she were nothing. Killing was in my nature. This was the point where I became most dangerous. When there is true love, this is the last thing you would expect to hear, but I was insane and I wanted to push the boundaries of reality to its fullest point. I wanted to mess with the laws of peace and happiness as much as I had the ability to. It was in my nature, nothing meant anything to me, and I made it a point to feel that way. To actually obtain happiness for a prolonged period of time was an illusion. I was probably the most deranged child the world has ever seen.

I am good at fitting in and bonding with people when I first meet them. But when it comes to having a place on this Earth, I have none. I have no real person to present to people. I eventually lose all joy and happiness in hanging out with the same friends. I need new ones to victimize. Gain friendship and kill later so I have no attachment towards anyone, so I will be ready for my self-riotous suicide when the time comes.

One time during my early childhood years, I remember watching TV and thinking of all the bad stuff I did. After committing a lot of evil comes a sense of satisfaction, a bizarre sense of feeling alive. The feeling comes and goes randomly. While I watched TV, and experienced this, I saw a man and a woman walking towards the house from outside my window. They were each holding a strait jacket by its sides as they walked in my house. They wanted to tie me up and throw me in a mental institution so I could get some perspective as to what I was doing in my life. I walked outside towards them and they yelled, “Come here.”

I laughed and looked at them, there was no way they were going to take me. “No, you’re shit, don’t take me.” They couldn’t force me into the jacket because I was too wild. They tried to catch me but they couldn’t come within one foot of me because of the energy I was giving off. They both gave me a look of disgust and walked away. I just laughed at what had happened and quickly repressed the whole incident.

Special people from all over the country were moved to my town. So, the actions I performed were dealt with more easily; people were less hurt. There were people that I wouldn’t get along with and people that I just couldn’t kill. “Mom, Alfred is gay.”

“It’s okay,” she said.

“Okay good then.” I instantly felt better. “He’s shit, gay people are shit.”

“No, Ali they are not.”

“Mom would you love me more if I were not gay?”

“No, I would love you the same.”

“Mom, you would love me just a tiny, tiny, bit more if I were not gay, right?”

"No, Ali, it does not mean anything." I knew however, that deep down inside, although she would never say it, that she would love me that tiny bit more if I were straight. I made my mind that I would never say I'm gay, because they are inferior. At such a young age I was asking questions only adults would ask. My mom was open to me being gay.

I was a skinny kid at a young age. I rarely overate and was very disciplined. My mom just wanted me to be happy, and she thought that maybe not eating enough food caused my depression. She went to the grocery store and bought unusually fatty foods and told me to eat away. *Wow, look at all this food*, I thought, *now I can just eat all through life and the pleasure of the food alone is sufficient to live happy*. Fat people are fat because they need more food than the average human to be happy. I saw a few of my fat friends eating three times as much as I could eat, and I would say, "Why do you eat that much?"

"I want to be happy!" one said, laughing.

I ate away and actually felt worse—physically and mentally slower. I was not meant to be fat. I found food to be my only enjoyment at a young age. After eating a normal healthy amount of food, I would eat more merely for the taste and thought to myself, *this is the only "pure" thing I enjoy*. Food in excess would not make me happy.

If reincarnation is true, we all have lived before, in many shapes and forms. Sometimes I think we all lived as dinosaurs. I sometimes dream of being a dinosaur, and in the back of my head I have a feeling that I was one before. I remember having the exact thought process that I do today, and I remember trying everything to live like a normal dinosaur. Physically I was the same but mentally I was not like the rest of them, not even close. But when I had to stand up on my own two feet it was impossible. At first I thought that finding another female dinosaur to mate with would be all that I would need. I found one through exhaustive searches and mated. She had a smile as if to ask, "What are you?" after we finished. She could not be a life-long companion.

Food, food is a guaranteed joy. As a dinosaur I just wanted to stay alive somehow, so if I just sat with a pile of food all day I would never be depressed. I ate and got a little fat. It only bought me more time to live. I looked around later and all the other dinosaurs looked at me like I was from Mars. I knew the truth; food would not be the answer. There was no answer, so I began to self-destruct. It took days, and all I would do I stand in one place, questioning why I would even move until it got to the point of why would I even eat. I experienced feelings of sorrow that would be incomprehensible to other dinosaurs; they all just gazed in fear at me, until I died. I roared as loud as a dinosaur could holding my head back. Shock waves of energy were sent everywhere, causing earthquakes and natural disasters. One dinosaur after another dropped, until they were all extinct. Yes, sometimes I actually think they were all extinct. Yes, sometimes I actually think this happened, but I know it's a delusion, I think.

Chapter 5

As a kid you are surrounded by your loved ones and are usually happy. Life and school have little pressure, and everyone is friendly. However, as each year after elementary and junior high school passes, you get closer and closer to facing the real world. Who you are starts becoming a question that you must deal with. A glimpse of the future starts to form.

While in high school, I realized the cohesiveness and order of my younger days had started to fade. I lost what little sanity I had, as I found myself surrounded by so many people. I started to think maybe I had some problems with not really fitting in. I began to become super shy, thinking that everything I'd say was something a "Dork" would say. I was okay until I started to smoke weed with my good friend Marshall, and that's when the real trouble came. Weed is a drug that expands your mind, and you begin to think of things you'd never thought of before, or at least that you've forgotten you have.

My thoughts became very real, and I thought to myself, Whoa, I'm a person. I was experiencing my first clear thoughts. Before smoking weed, I had thought that all I needed out of life was a girlfriend, a lot of money, a good car, and a big house, and as long as I had these things I'd be a success. But I realized true success comes from within. Without a true love for yourself, you can never be happy. Having all the money in the world, a girlfriend, a nice car, a big house would all be meaningless. Most rich people aren't even happy. A lower income worker, who truly enjoys his or her existence, is more of a success than an unhappy millionaire. Those are the facts of life. Material possessions usually make you temporarily happy, but then the desire to want more comes, so inner peace is never obtained. The true meaning of life is to be happy, to love yourself, and love someone else; money and material objects are needed bit not to the extent that society places them.

The first few times I smoked weed were fun because I didn't know what was going on. Then I started to think. I actually stopped thinking of other people thought, and started to delve into myself. *I am a person, stop being a dork, have fun*, is what I thought. I let go of initial plan of becoming wealthy and having a girlfriend. I felt good, *why even place that burden on you*? All that was left was I. I was the only thing I had, and I started to learn who I was. I looked within myself, and drew a blank. I felt nothing but existence. There was nobody inside of me.

My next thought was to follow my body and thoughts. I withdrew from conversations, and became a blank slate, mostly every view I had was illogical. Oh my God, I'm crazy, is what I thought. Some basic universal thoughts were entering my head, such as, *Nothing means anything. All life is, is who you are, and liking yourself.* Who was I? Life, I feel today, is just a bunch of beliefs; all my beliefs at the time were full of shit. They were all negative. The normal human has a basic set of beliefs and viewpoints that make the person who they are. The person's beliefs are something sacred, and intangible asset. Being a human is a beautiful thing. One can argue with another person about his or her beliefs, but compassion and love for one is usually always present – this is what I consider practicing happiness.

I started to dislike smoking weed. It became a chore. Why didn't I like it? I should be motivated to project, or a test, when others were happy? I smoked it anyway. I had no will power. Every time I did it, I would think crazier and crazier thoughts. My personality changed every ten minutes as I desperately tried to find common ground, yet I never had a common reality. My realities and thought processes are completely different from whoever I'm with. Each reality lasts about ten seconds in a conversation, and ten minutes alone. Some philosophers argue my same point saying that your reality changes every second of every day; however, when I speak of reality I speak of me knowing what the hell's going on. Where I am, and how I'm supposed to feel, are the questions of my reality.

I desperately tried not to think of myself, and to hop into someone else's brain, trying to get a glimpse of what it's like to be human. *Wow, who cares*, is what I got life is supposed to be. *Life is too precious and beautiful to worry, but you have to like yourself.* This I cannot genuinely do. How can I love someone when I can't love myself? I have nothing to love; it's mentally impossible. One would argue for me to take a class in Psychology and learn how to be happy. I do agree with that viewpoint. I can be happier and today, through a tremendous amount of suffering and medicine, I have changed. However, things cannot change that mush. There is something called, "The facts of life, and who you are." Change is possible, but whatever does change is minimal in the long run. The conversations I am involved are usually fake. I only do them in order to not think of myself as normal, and ultimately to live. I guess that is all you can say I want. I want to live. I never want it to end. I may suffer more than anyone in the world, in such bizarre ways that not even a lobotomy would give me peace, but to actually die was the only thing I didn't want. At the age of my weed experimentation, I would have erratic joy at time, what felt like pure happiness. When you're down for a long time you usually come back up. I lived for the "up" periods.

My friend Marshall was a special person. His whole existence was being happy, and no matter what I did I couldn't make him unhappy. I tried to get philosophical with Marshall but he was not smart enough to talk about the insanity I dealt with. Marshall was telling me about a gay neighbor named Nick who would have answers for my questions. I always tried to avoid him, because I hated gay people. One day Marshall and I had gotten some psychedelic mushrooms. "Ali this is the only time we can do it," he said.

Not knowing what he meant I hesitantly said, "Okay." If I didn't like weed, how could I like mushrooms? Mushrooms are much stronger than weed. The first part of the trip was fun. I was happy. I thought only happy thoughts and was thinking, *What was I thinking before, being so negative all the time? Life is fun, and is meant to be enjoyed.* This lasted maybe two hours. Then I looked at a view of the whole city, and was pushed down mentally. *Why?* I thought, referring to why are we all here.

I explained this to Marshall, and he said, "Ali we all get that." I felt better for a second but then I got the thought that he was not for real. I kept delving into every situation I was ever in, and thought how none of it mattered, and everything was bullshit. This is common in a lot of teenagers, but I thought I was the only one. Every family friend I had ever had meant nothing to me, and I couldn't accept it. I was as unhappy as can be. What was supposed to do? "Ali, you're gay." Marshall said.

"I'm not gay." I responded.

"Ali, I'm gay." Marshall said. I had no answer. I had been a friend with him for over eight or nine years and I had no reaction to him saying he was gay. "Ali, you're crazy!" he said.

"I'm not crazy," I said. Marshall had a look like he didn't know what to do. He was still happy; he felt nothing like me, because what is so bad about life? He mentally could not get to my level and I had tried everything.

"Ali, let's go talk to Nick.:

We went next store, and Nick approached us and said, "I'm going to go to a concert tonight." *Wow*, I thought, *this guy is a bad-ass.* He pulled out a huge bag of weed, and we all started smoking it. Every second I went through was painful. So, I had to break the pain.

"So, you're gay?" I asked,

"Yes" Nick said laughing.

"No, you're not gay." I said.

"What?" he smiled.

"You're too bad-ass. You can get girls. Why don't you just go out there and get girls, have sex all day." I said. He laughed hysterically,

I was saying, "Girls are the best things in the world, and you hate everything they do and say. Gay people look at girls, and don't think they are attractive, you'd rather look at guys and have sex all day."

"You don't think I want to have sex with girls when I look at them? They are beautiful. I don't like them," Nick said. "I love girls, I don't want to hurt them." He said laughing, "What's wrong with being gay?"

"All gay people are bums and all they do is sit at home and think about shit and condoms!"

"No, I'm happy!"

"You might as well fuck me." I said.

He did. "I love you!" he said laughing hysterically.

"Why don't you just talk to guys, and when it comes to sex just go out and get a hooker?"

"I've had a girlfriend. I wasn't happy,"

"Geese you just live your life like you're the best person in the world." I said. He laughed. "Don't be gay," I said.

"I love you," he repeated.

Marshall viewing the whole thing then spoke and said, "Ali there's nothing wrong with being gay" I felt a love for myself feeling absolutely insane. I wanted all attention. "There are smart people that look over what you are doing."

"There are?" I said laughing gladly.

"Ali, they don't even want me to give you weed, let alone mushrooms," he said. I felt like I owned both their souls and I loved the feeling of being I total control.

"I'm going to kill you," Nick said. I thought to myself, *Shit, this guy would actually do it*. "I'm going to kill you," he repeated laughing while getting a gun.

"But what about your future? You're going to go to jail."

"I don't care what happens to me, I'm going to kill you."

"Geese you're so bad-ass," I said and, feeling like a little kid who's gotten away with stealing a candy bar, I walked out the door.

An average human would have shot himself, but he wasn't average. All their dreams and everything they believed in was destroyed. I would not stay with the person and love them. Who were they to love now? This person was so strong he did not kill himself. I left the house and went from thinking I owned the world back to being a stupid kid. Immediately I became stupid, not even knowing what had just happened. *What is it?* I thought. I had learned nothing from the incident that just happened, but whatever it was I would strive to do again.

I sat in deep depression on Marshall's couch trying to watch TV. I felt so depressed that Sigmund Freud could not have helped me. Now that I look at it, I feel that no one was psychotic enough to feel as I did—not even people who committed suicide. It took nine or ten hours to get back to my idea of feeling normal. Without knowing it I went out the next day with all my evil habits in place.

I'd later look for the fittest and most special people to try to be with. My mentality was one where I asked myself, *Why should I even hang out with someone who is normal?* They were losers just as most of the population was. I would be a happy man to knock out all the winners, so I (a loser) would feel special.

School took most of my wariness away as I acted out my role of being superhuman in the classroom. There was sex in many of my classes. Besides flat out killing someone, I think sex in class is one of the rarest things that can happen in school. When sex did take place in class, people wither had a blank look, a look of confusion, or a look of laughter on their faces. In a Chemistry class for instance, I fucked a girl thinking, I'd be happy just being with her, but the pleasure left and I would reassure myself that I was the worst human being ever to live. I had all attention in the class. People would laugh at how crazy I was, and I would dish out some more hate-enabling for them to like me. "At least let us like you!" I shook my head thinking *everything sucks no matter what.* I would not let myself feel joy, it was too much for me.

I then looked at the teacher and said, "Come on, join in."

He simply responded, "I hate myself." He would in no way participate in the sex. I then noticed an Asian person who looked in some way different.

"Who is this guy?" I yelled.

With his head shaking back and forth in haste, and a smile, he said, "I'm the smartest kid in the world."

"Come on lets have sex!"

"No," he said hastily.

"Come on," I repeated.

"No" he said again. I could tell this guy was really thinking. He did look intelligent. It was almost as tough he was trained for this moment, and I just gave up. I was then usually sent to the principal where I also got him.

"You know most of the students here are idiots, you hate some of them but have to try to act nice. Sometimes you just want to tell them to fuck off." I said.

"I love you," he laughed. Every time I would come to the principal's office "high," I would just shower him with compliments that made him feel exceptional. He laughed and tried to stay away from me, and said, "I love this guy." He couldn't do anything. He could not tell me to follow any instructions or rules, because I was more powerful than he was. All the personal and staff around me told me to check into a mental institution. *I'm not crazy*, I thought. I didn't see anything wrong with me. If anything, I felt smarter than they were. I felt as though they should ask me questions about their own personal lives.

As I write this now, I've been keeping long-term friends. I now try to do everything in my power not to think crazy thoughts, such as, *This person is just here to stop me from killing other people and keep me in control. He is an actor*. These thoughts stop all the fun I have with the individual.

There was a moment of time where I thought I had the whole school under my wings. I would walk around feeling like nobody, and then for an instant saw who I really was, and how I fit in the school. I felt like Satan, and I felt I had everyone's souls within me. Sadly, I didn't have my own. So, what did this all mean? I had nothing. I'd go to parties at the age of fifteen and act foolish. I was consistently trying to ruin every situation with bad mental energy. I remember one person saying, "Why are you doing this?" I had no answer and could only call him shit, for no one was as good as me.

Gary was a friend I met in a summer school biology class. I was taking the class with the attitude of acting it. This was one of my realities, to move forward in school and feel like a regular student. As long as I did this, I would be okay. I could hide behind a mask, and consistently move forward with the rest of the people my age. This was the only thing that made me think I was normal. I would shove all the sexual confusion in the back of my head, as though it was not real.

Chapter 6

I became somewhat good friends with Gary. He would ask me if I did the homework, and what I did last weekend. I kept up a shield for a long time, but then, I tried to mentally rearrange him. The confusion took over. "Gary, are you gay?" He gave no answer. I feel like shit, because I knew this wasn't an appropriate question to ask. I would forget about this and the next day I asked, "Am I gay?"

He responded, "Well, do you like girls?"

"No," I said in confusion. At the time I did not even know if I liked them. "Gay people aren't human," I said.

"What is wrong with it? I'm happy," he said.

"So, you are a person. Yeah I can see, you are a person," I said. I looked with all my intelligence into him and saw a normal person, a person whose life's goal was to be happy and to avoid suffering. I got a glimpse of his inner self, his personality. He was a person with behaviors just like everyone else, but he was gay. I know today that being gay does not make a person that much different from everyone else. It is the least big deal in the world.

I noticed, however, that my problem was not cut-and-dry, I had a load that makes an in-the-closet gay person feel like the Dalai Lama. On the outside Gary and I may have looked similar, with both of us having a healthy body and face. But on the inside, I saw that we were nothing alike. I asked him if I could see a person inside of me. "Yes, you are a person." He said. This gave me joy.

"Am I gay?" I asked.

"Yeah, I think you're gay."

"But there are so few of us."

"No" he said, "There are a lot of us."

I looked inside myself, and could only think of the crazy sex stories. I got him to believe the stories. Suddenly we felt more and more unlike each other. He began to know me. I then asked him to analyze me and speak of my future, because I had no clue of to what it would hold. All I saw inside me was life for the next six or seven years and nothing past that. I wondered why. The sexual behavior and murder could only last so long. After that was through, I felt my life was basically through.

"Oh my God, I'm crazy," I said. He agreed. "I have to kill myself after six or seven years," I said, or else life would really suck. All I would do is think of what I have done. I wouldn't be ignorant. There would be no joy. I want to go out a legend. Whom will I have sex with?"

He named many people and some people he said stuck out in my mind. "There are some Italian guys you'll love. You'll fuck all of them. There is a big one, you're especially going to love." (He referred to Anthony; who was moved to live near me). I had seen him before and I would have to get him; he had all the qualities I wanted.

"I'm going to get a nose job and have sex with my plastic surgeon." I said.

Gary looked at me with amazement that I would plan such a thing. "Yes Ali, this will happen, you're going to regret not staying with him. He will have a lot of money."

I kept saying to myself, Stay with the surgeon, because after that there will be little joy. He would be one of my last victims. I must remember to say yes to live with him when the time comes. "I want to get the president," I told Gary.

"Yes, the president is very tempting, but you know that there are too many people you'd have to go through to get to him." Gary said. It's true the president is too well protected for me to try and kill. "You'll work at Lisa's," (that was a local deli), "a lot of sex will take place. There will be a gay guy there, and you're going to love him. There will also be a straight guy there you're going to love. You're going to hurt a lot of people, you're even going to hurt girls," he went on.

"I'm going to U.S.C." I said.

"They'll be ready for you at U.S.C., you're already in," he went on.

"I'm going to kill myself during U.S.C." I said.

"You're not going to kill yourself," Gary replied.

"How did you know?"

"Because I know you," Gary said.

"When is it all going to end?" I asked.

He looked straight at me as if to read me and said, "You'll kill yourself, probably when you're 35 and you find yourself all alone, fat, and unhappy."

"You're going to go through life having two or three boyfriends and be happy." I said.

"How do you know this?" he asked just as I did.

"I know you," I said, "You love people. I wish I could love people the way you can.

Gary said, "Yeah, and I wish I could like people the way you can."

I said, "You'll love Jim Morrison and The Doors. You'll know some people at this school who will attend college in Santa Barbara. You'll love Santa Barbara; a lot of events take place there. You're a legend in Santa Barbara. You'll start watching classic movies. You'll love the *Godfather*. And in the movie *Lawrence of Arabia*, you'll hear the main character say the line, 'nothing is written.' You'll even use that line. You'll start to smoke weed, you don't like weed. You will just drink most of the time. You're not gay, you just love girls so much that you don't want to mess with them psychologically, as you do to guys." Just as Satan is gay in the "South Park" television show.

All these problems can be read off my mind. In reality we all have our problems that we must deal. Anyone who says they don't ever worry, with the exclusion of only a handful of holy people, is lying.

There was one person named Jim who was different from others. I felt that he'd live the most successful life in our school. In high school his popularity was average, and he was very smart academically. The guy had perfect responses to everything I'd say, and had the most peaceful confidence I'd ever seen. It seemed as though he had the same mental attitude I did towards everything. This is just because he saw my point of view in life and respected it. Most people cannot share my mental point of view because they don't know what it is. I don't even know what it is, however at the time I could act as crazy or depressed as I wanted and he'd still act the same. He was a good person who could mentally connect with everything I'd say. When I asked the typical, "Did you," he just said, "Yeah," and walked away. I didn't care for his response and he didn't care enough about my question that it was worth talking about.

"You're going to have a lot of good times with Jim, you two will drink all the time," Gary said.

"Look at Jim, he's so bad-ass" I said.

"Yes, we like Jim," Gary said, referring to himself and his two gay friends.

"You want to have sex with him," I said.

"Yes, we do," he replied.

Jim was a character who was real; he let anyone like him," I said.

"Yes, we do," he replied.

Jim was a character who was real; he let anyone like him, but was not gay---just how I thought I was.

"You're going to become really good friends with Jim. You're later going to become really good friends with Jim. You're later going to hurt him," Gary said.

"Yeah, but will it still be the same?" I asked, meaning good times after accepting who I am, and breaking his heart.

"No, you'll still have good times, but it won't be the same."

I was getting excited for the future, what it will hold, how it core would be. All the hiding that I have been doing all my life will come out. I was to experience a lot of life. An adventure was in my future; I just had to keep in mind that it must someday end and I should take advantage of the possessions that I can obtain. I told Gary how he and I should be together forever and then I thought I'd be at peace. He accepted, "Okay, Ali we will be together forever." I was happy for a few moments, knowing that I had someone's heart and soul to forever play with.

I met his two friends Gerald and Mitch, and I'd contribute to the conversation that they were involved in. I changed the conversation mood from glad to sadness. *What is it?* I thought. I felt like shit after everything I'd say. "Sorry guys I'm a dork!" I said. I thought of myself as someone who was not socially cool, and this was the reason I couldn't communicate with harmony.

"No, it's okay Ali, we like you," they'd say.

While sitting in our lab groups for Biology, I saw Gary, Gerald, and Mitch in a group laughing. I walked up to them and shyly spoke hate, the language my tongue was used to. I stood there in hesitation not knowing what to do after I spoke.

"Ali, you're a dork!" Mitch said. They all laughed and I walked away. I then thought of my reality of how I had to ace school.

"I'm smart," I told Gary.

"You're not smart" he said laughing.

"No, I really am. Watch, I'll study hard for this next test and I'll get an A."

He responded as if to say, "Show me what you've got." I got less than half the questions right on the exam, while the class average was a B. It was too hard to accept that I wasn't book smart. There are many other people just like me who have similar qualities except one thing, their intelligence. Intelligence is what gets you places in life.

Take Tim Leary for example, he was a wacko who was book smart. "Tune in, turn on, and drop out?" This is silly. He graduated from Harvard, and held a prestigious job teaching. Through continuous drug use he became more and more crazy. It is said that after ingesting LSD three times you are legally insane. He used his intelligence along with personal philosophies to sell a countless number of books, and intervene with many other people's lives. He wrote all his books in order to find other people like him. His writings hurt more people than they helped. In fact, he barely helped anyone. He was just interesting, as I am. He wanted to know who he was deep down to the core. If you're crazy, your core makes no sense. But he found a handful of people who shared similar thoughts to his and this made him happy. They just united as a group and, as hard as it was, he and a group of rare people found each other and a place in this world.

However, I feel that there is nobody like me. Maybe someday I'll run into a clone and we'd share similar thoughts, but that is highly unlikely. I wish I were smart because it would make life a lot easier. I do, however, possess a high emotional intelligence. I always know what the other person is thinking about me. And I have rare bursts of words that make people trip out in the wisdom of them.

Once I realized that I was not book smart, I immediately got depressed, thinking, *Why am I in school? Why am I even trying? It's meaningless. I am doing wrong to the world. I should be going to Church and straightening my life up*. I received a barely passing grade in the Biology class, My realities were spinning without control. I felt that I must do something.

Time passed and I completely did not care for Gary and his friends, and at the last day of class Gary said, "Ali, do you want to go to the fair with us?"

"No, I'm kind of busy." I said.

"Ali you're coming to the fair with us," he demanded.

"Okay" I said. We walked five feet and I said to the three of them, "You want to have sex with me! Why else would we go? Can I suck your dicks?" I did Gerald, and Gary at the same time, and said to Gerald, "No, you're not gay, why do you hang around these guys? Oh, it's because you're afraid of being alone." His face agreed with everything I said. "You're shit!" I felt incredible.

Mitch pulled out a gun, and fearfully said, "I'm going to kill you!" He had it right to my head.

"No," I yelled. All three faces were astonished with the power of my words.

"Then I'm going to kill myself."

As Mitch aimed the gun towards his head, ready to pull the trigger I yelled, "No, don't kill yourself!" He gave a look like he was disappointed and bewildered. The other faces were filled with astonishment.

"Why are you doing this?" Mitch said in a tone of voice that I'm not sure he has ever used.

"There's nothing else to do!" I replied. He almost went crazy himself when he heard me say that. "Mitch did you…" I asked.

"" Yeah, there's nothing else to do!" he said in pain and laughter."

"See I'm like Mitch," I said to the others.

"I feel like shit right now," he responded, as if to say "How and why do you live like this?" He had never experienced a pain as strong as the one I showed him. I smiled and walked away; where I went and where I was going I did not know.

I went through various groups of friends still experimenting with drugs, and tried to act how a person "my age," would act. Everything felt unnatural. I was waiting however to hit the age where I could hang out with Jim. When the times of experimenting with drugs was over, I had to hang out with people who I thought to be high school partiers. I wanted to be socially accepted and try to meet everyone, and build my name up as a mogul. During my last year of high school, I became good friends with Jim.

"Did you…"

"Yeah," is all he would say and walk away.

"Did you…"

"Yeah."

The answers were so simple, this is all I want when I ask the, "Did you" questions. I didn't care to mean my questions in a gay way, I was just curious, and Jim's one-word responses to every queer question I could ask made me think he was like me. Simple, and smart, with the attitude of, "Why would I care?" *Jesus this guy can understand me*. He was the first person that I could ever communicate with on a consistent level. *I can love and hate this guy to death and he still wouldn't care about what he's doing*. He head was always straight. My head however was a walking case study.

Sometimes I don't even know how I made it to his house to hang out. What I think makes a good person is when you accept the fact that a man can love another man, and not worry about whether what you're doing is morally right. There is no limit to platonic love. I made Jim feel like a god when we hung out, and he was still modest. Jim and I referred to ourselves as the "two best people in the world." "I mean, come on Ali, how could there ever be two better guys than us to live?" Jim said.

All I would do is shower him with all my insane love, and he would accept it. Sometimes he even dished the love out in the same level as I gave. It was pure. Love is something that two people share and it's limitless. Be it two people from different worlds, love has its own language. It is universal, and takes away all worry. Love is the most powerful force on the planet, and keeps all of us going. I never thought that I'd ever experience so much closeness with another person. I don't think any two people in history have experienced what we had. The friendship did not consist of sexual relations. That made the love even stronger. When it came down to sex we both shared similar views. Physical lust we both did not understand. The idea seemed unnatural. It would ruin the love we had. The idea seemed unnatural. It would ruin the love we had. It was during these few years in life were I was happiest.

Jim and I would drink, eat, talk about money, and discuss our love and hate towards the world. I performed well enough in school to make it into U.S.C. School of Business, and I was skinny. All I would need now is a girlfriend and I'd be perfect. I worked hard my whole life to get to that period. Today, however I don't understand how I became so happy. It felt so simple at the time. What goes up must come down. I will explain how I slowly lost everything.

Chapter 7

During the time after high school, I started to work at a pizza deli, named Lisa's, close to home. I met may unique individuals there. I can think of none who was an average Joe. One straight guy had such a sense of self-confidence that I loved him right away. Different chemical balancing in the brain is what made him who he is. Some people are just born naturally happier than others. What a shame, why did God do this only to some people and not everyone.?

"Everything has always come easy to me," he would say, "and when it comes to girls, confidence is the most important thing." Joe was hired around the same time I was, so we were both new to the place. We started cracking jokes to one another. We laughed at each other for the whole shift. This is how I initially bond to most people

I meet. We sat at a break, and he points to his crotch, and says, "Do you want to suck my dick?"

I was shocked, "Oh, is that why?" Nothing went through my head that whole shift. I was just trying to keep up with the conversation in order to feel normal.

"Yeah, why else?" he said.

"What have you heard about me?" I asked.

"I heard you were stupid."

"Yeah, I'm stupid." I said laughing.

"How stupid are you?" he asked with disbelief.

"Ohh, I'm really stupid."

"Forget it, you don't have to." So, I forgot about it for a while, and days passed where all I would talk about is money, stealing, and deep love.

"Did you…" I asked.

"I went…"

I asked him stupid questions too, like where in the world are we and what was the standard way to think? Complete madness is all that came through my mouth. I felt he was so special that I had to steal his soul. We would have conversations like those that Jim and I had. Joe spoke as a bright person with a true sense of confidence and God damn! He was sincere.

I tried to match his thinking, and for a split second it was there, his reality. His life was filled with joy and happiness, and he enjoyed it all. Life was fun for him. "That is the worst thing," I said referring to a cook messing up an order. Joe's mother was seated right next to me, she overheard that comment and I looked over and saw her laugh. "You know?" I said referring to who I am.

"I don't know how you can live with yourself," she said, while nodding her head back and forth.

I tried to get serious, "I'm not a person." I said

"You are a person, why are you here?"

I thought for a second and realized she was right. We might as well have sex!" I said.

"Okay, where?" she said.

I took her to the ladies' bathroom in the back, where we started intercourse, and I said, "You're from the best family ever." She laughed. I adored her whole family. She was a church-going woman who was pure. "You're beautiful." I said to her next. Thein I said,

"You're shit." I felt as though I was Satan fucking God. I loved the pureness of God, but I could never be pure, Satan had a hold of me, and I loved him. I calmly finished the sex, and I felt emptiness inside me, followed by a rush that heroin could not beat. I left her for garbage, when I had just changed her life forever.

I went back to my state of confusion worse than ever. *Where am I going in life? What does all this sex mean? Am I a devil without a cause? Am I meant to start a revelation? What's my grand purpose for being here?* I went back to doing the duties required for the job, came home, greeted my family with an unusual enthusiasm after feeling that I killed someone, and my family would greet me faces of anger and disgust, as if to ask what I was doing with my life.

A day later Joe was next to me. Wow, he would be a good one to get, I thought. "Did you…" this time I did not walk away after the question.

He asked, "Do you want to suck my dick?" I said yes and in the back I told him he had the "best confidence in the world." I told him he was gay, I told him he was shit.

"Ali," he said with a face of a person who needed something so badly you'd do anything for it. His face was one of such deep love that it is unfathomable. "Ali, let me fuck you."

"You're shit," I said again. I then walked slowly back inside the store, not understanding what I did.

"Ali, let me fuck you," he said again.

"Okay, I'll let you," I said, and I walked back in.

A short while later I was accepted to U.S.C. I actually cried. It was the greatest accomplishment I had achieved. I put a countless number of hours in at studying. I told all my friends of my accomplishment, and felt I was managing my life the best that I could. While still at my junior college I would go to U.S.C. parties, drink, and have fun.

Anthony is someone who I secretly loved. I had a feeling he loved me also but I did not know it. I looked at him as if he was a god; we had barely spoken to one another because I was so afraid of how bad-ass and socially popular he was. If I were to talk to him I would not know what to say. I thought of him as the best Italian in the world.

One night at U.S.C. party I saw him filling drinks at a keg. I had to say something or I'd feel crazy, "Bullshit party." I said, thinking the whole world thought as I thought, and with his philosophy background, he'd understand and agree. He said something right back to me, which I did not understand. I did the fake laugh that I'm so good at and I walked away and continued drinking. The time came for another refill and I was scared of seeing him again with nothing to say. In fear I walked up to him with a smile, trying to avoid social awkwardness. We were both trying to show that on the outside we liked one another.

He then said with a meaningful, and humoring look, "Why are you here?"

I laughed and thought, *Oh shit, let the showdown begin*. It was as if we knew each other for our whole lives, just waiting to talk to each other.

"My friends all treat me like I'm a god," he said as I laughed. "Ali, you have no place on this Earth." I had a look of sorrow to the degree that my life would never have anything stable, and meaningful. "You have no place on planet Mars!" Not only did I have no place with other people, I also had no place living by myself. I would self-destruct, acting out actions that someone who is possessed would. "I love you," he said.

I responded, "You're going to make sooo much money, you're going to drive a BMW." I felt as though he were my creation.

"I know, and I'm doing it for you!" he said. We both then felt a force of downward pressure afflicting us, as if the devil was present. "Ali, you can have your millions. Write this stuff down!" My only language was of money and how much of it I wanted to make. Money was my God. He continued, "My dog is smarter than you!" he said.

"What do you do, when you see your dog when coming home?" I asked. I was curious about how you should treat your dog. I can't even get along with mine.

"I come home, greet him, give him food and go on with what I'm supposed to be doing," was his answer.

"Oh, just like you love your dog, but like yourself more!" I said. He gave out a laugh. I then said, "No, I'm smart, listen." I tried using all my possible brainpower thinking of something brilliant, and said, "People sometimes forget to say help to their friends."

"You just said you love me," he said with love.

There was a pause, "You're shit," I said hesitantly.

"I feel like shit right now!" he said.

"Anthony you're the Godfather, you're the best, toughest possible person there can be!" I said He was a winner and everything he tried at turned out successful. He constantly had beautiful girl friends.

"Ali, I'm gay," he said.

"No, gay people get a snarl when they laugh," meaning a certain form of the nose. "You don't, you're too bad-ass." I said. There was no way I'd accept that he was gay.

"My brothers and I have fucked each other!" he said referring to the meaning that I places on sexual relations. The brothers fucked each other to see what could be so bad about my life. They saw nothing. "We sucked each other's dicks in philosophy class talking about you!" he said.

"Go like this," I said. I put my hand in the air and pretended as if I'm petting a dog. I couldn't even do that without asking myself the question, *Why?* My form was terrible. He did it with style. "See you're the best at everything!" I said. I thought of the future and told him, "I'm going to kill myself." I meant that I was going to end my life in the near future, not that night,

"No, I'll kill myself," he said.

I can't have this guy kill himself, I thought. I'm going to be in a mental institution. I'll ask to see you, come visit me. But what are you going to do? You'll be right next to my parents when you see me!" I had assumed that my visitors would see me all at once. "How will you act? How are you going to stand in place?" This was the last thing someone like him would worry about, but to me it's the most important thing. "You're so bad-ass it doesn't matter!" I said.

"I love you," he replied. "Ali, you're the most interesting person in the world! he said.

"Okay, then I'm going to be in an institution forever." This really is where I should be. Everyone would be happier without me. "You're going to visit me in there all the time."

"I will, I'll visit you all the time. I'll write down notes about your actions." Being a philosophy major, he'd have a lot of questions.

"You might as well fuck me!" I said. He did and I asked him, "Jeese, how smart are you?"

"Ali, I'm one of the smartest people in the world!"

"Tell me something philosophy related." I thought that was the only true knowledge.

"…" he said with ease.

"Who cares!" I said. It did not matter, he laughed hysterically, knowing what a joke life really is. The sex was finished, and I stood up and said, "Wait." I then French kissed him, and said, "Who cares!" The whole gay thing was in reality such a joke. There is nothing wrong with being gay. There is something wrong with being crazy.

He had so many questions to ask me. "Why did you go to the gym so much?" he asked because at that time I went every day for two or three years hating it. It seemed like this guy knew everything about me. Then I started to think of me, what I've done to him, and the world. If I had stayed there I would have cried. I walked away and looked back. I saw a combination of love, hate, and confusion in his eyes.

"What---where are you going?" he said in confusion. I did not know why but I proceeded and looked back and he yelled, "Why would you care?" loud enough for me to hear. That made sense to me.

Why would I care? I thought. I saw him laugh to himself hysterically while his pants were still down. I nodded, "Yeahh" to him. We connected with the insanity. While walking off I heard, "He was the last one," as if to say, "What have you done, you're hopeless." Everyone in the party knew who I was. Without me knowing it, I was famous. I got my friends and left the party. The event was not discussed. My energy was so powerful that they or I could not remember what had just happened.

Jim and I frequently got drunk and went to a local food joint called Nancie's. While eating, I looked to the table next to me and it was Nick (who lived next store to my old friend Marshall) seated with two other adult men. I remembered his face, "Nick!" I said, as though he was an old friend, "How are you?" He replied saying he was okay. He had a serious look on his face while I was speaking to him. I don't remember what I said to him, but I remember talking nonstop for three minutes straight. I thought since he was gay, he would understand me. I tried to tell him about old times, and how I used to be depressed and I was better now. I was telling him my philosophies on life. I heard no response, so I said, "What do you think?" I knew he had something to say, but that he was just shy or scared to talk to me.

His face turned from seriousness to anger, as he said, "You're savior of the human race." I had no idea who I was and what he was talking about. He proceeded, "Ali, what happened that day I met you, I fucked you." All I could remember was going to his house on mushrooms and how I had a bad trip. I was in denial about the sex ever taking place. "I hate you," he said.

"But what about all that talking I was doing?" I thought with all that talking I did, that I was normal, and not an unusual person.

"I don't understand what you're talking about, you're queer, and look at who you're hanging out with, the President of the United States."

"Jim?" I said, as I looked at him.

"Ali, I don't know," he said in a joking way. Our waitress even looked at me in misery as I was talking to Nick. Everyone knew who I was. I said a few other things to Nick. Everyone knew who I was. I said a few other things to Nick, and his friends. Pure love followed by coldness that shocks people.

One person said, "I can never love again." How many people had I dine this to? "And you've given gay people such a bad name. What is soooo bad about being gay?" Nick asked.

I couldn't think of one reason. "We might as well be together," I said laughing, "And we'll take you." I thought for a moment and said, "Jim, let's go." The car ride home with Jim was different. I was not stupid anymore. At that moment I knew who I was. Everything I would usually say was denied by the truth. *I'm savior of the human race.* I would think, *Jim's going to be President.* These thoughts scared me and there was complete silence the whole way home. This is how our conversations would be if I told myself the truth. All the fun would end. I quickly tried to forget what happened and within a couple of days everything was back to normal.

At Lisa's, Anthony had a brother named Don. He was a co-worker of mine; he was a sort of angry person, yet very confident. Like Anthony, he was socially popular. He always had a sense of what was going on. I eventually found out that he was the same Don I got to at a Metallica concert at an early age. So, he tried to be very friendly. I thought that I had to compete with him to see who was a better person. Some people view life as a human rat. Everyone tries to do their best to outperform one another and be on top, without ever having an end in sight. I took this theory to an extreme, the wrong way, and applied it to friendships. I would join friendly conversations as though we were talking to see who the "better" person was.

"Yeah, me and my friends were drinking in Tijuana and were chilling," someone might say.

Building on the topic, I would interrupt with an authoritative voice, "I went to Tijuana with my friends and I lost my wallet." Silence, no one could connect with me. I was better than them; I tried to outdo their comments, as though I were above them. Sometimes people would even laugh at me. When I did this to Don, he would even laugh at me, he would get angry and walk away from the conversation. I tried to avoid every social situation so he would not find out I'm fake.

A man named Rick, Don, and I were talking. "I'm going to the country fair tomorrow," Rick said.

"Yeah" Don said. "The fair should be fun."

They looked at me as if to ask, "Who are you?"

The first thing that came to my mind was that I was the best person.

"I'm going to go the fair and walk in for free." I basically said I was better than the both of them. Rick had no clue, but Don knew what I meant, and made an angry face and walked off. *Oh no*, I thought, *he doesn't like me*. Quickly I had to think of something so that he would love me. As he was leaving, "Don, did you get the delivery?"

"Yeah," he nodded with anger.

"Did you…"

"Yeah," he said again with anger. I wanted his soul. He still tried his best to like me, but without really knowing it I tried to bring him down, in every situation. I could see hate in his eyes.

A conversation of smoking weed came up. "I hate weed," I said "it's the worst thing." Saying this is like saying you hate yourself, because weed brings your true self out. "Here is the thought that always gets me, they take hormones from a cow…" That was not what I was talking about. I played with his mind so much, he hated me. The next thing I thought was to ask, "Suck your dick?"

"I don't love you," he said. A few more lines of hate disbursed between the two of us, and were off to our normal duties. He looked and said, "Ali, I'll let you suck it!"

Yeah, I thought, *I'm cool.* "Let's go outside." As we were walking I told him how he was and how he is just meant to raise his eyebrows and jump over walls. Stupid humor really, but it was funny to me. He laughed slightly.

I started the action, and he said with hate, "No, you're not gay."

"How did you know?" I said laughing.

"What is so bad about being gay?" he said with anger. He started to get uppity, and restless. "You're savior of the human race, I hate you." He yelled.

"You're shit," I said.

"You're nobody, you're a walking joke, your only enjoyment in life is food. What are you thinking right now?"

I replied by telling him, "I'm singing the song, "You're Crazy' from Guns N Roses," and I laughed, feeling oh-so-powerful.

"You're as dumb as a fish! You're meant to jump in the water and be with the fish! Kill yourself." I laughed, he then said, "No, you're not stupid, you're the smartest guy in the world, you can't be killed! How did you make it this far? Ali, I'm going to kill myself."

"No, don't kill yourself," I said, "You're too badass. How smart are you?"

"Ali I'm one of the smartest people in the world."

"What else?" I said,

"Alright Ali, I love you." We then felt a mutual feeling in the air, our moods changed,

"What is that?" I asked. I now think it was a feeling of the reality around us, and how mood is in the air and how it dictates conversations, and behavior. Maybe this is God running the show.

"It can't be explained," he said. We went inside the store and my name came up to Joe again. "I love Ali, I'm going to marry Ali."

I laughed as I heard this, *See, look at what you are doing to people.* I laughed again; I loved laughing at these things. I thrive off being crazy. It is the only thing that really makes me laugh.

"No, it's not funny, you know what you're doing to people." Don was now dictating to me, and I was forced to listen to what he said; meanwhile I looked at Joe.

I said, "Joe did you…"

"I went…"

His eyes melted for the love that he had for me, I was playing him like a toy.

"No, you're not stupid anymore, stop it now," said Don. I thought of what it would be like to actually think of things that are not stupid to say. There was nothing. I have no real reason for being here. Being stupid at least gave me life.

The feeling of joyful insanity was still in the air the next day at work. As we sat down again, Don said, "Ali, I was at the Metallica concert in San Francisco." I didn't know what he meant. Remember I repress every sexual experience as though it never happened. "Ali, you sucked my dick at that concert. You sucked Anthony's dick too." I was thinking maybe to write some of this down, because this was the truth, and I have always been in a state of confusion. I knew I'd forget everything. But I didn't write anything. Don went on, "Ali we moved from San Francisco to be close to you. We had to pass so many tests and competed with so many other families to be with you and we were chosen to live by you. Metallica's music wasn't as powerful and vulgar before you."

This is true because Metallica has recently switched to playing softer music. The band eventually decided to forget about me and play their kind of music.

"And how is it you've never had a girlfriend?" he asked. "You are the most lovable person in the world." The truth is that I was not stupid around girls. I tried to avoid them to not play with them negatively. They are too precious. There is an abundance of guys who are less important that I chose to be my victims.

The same night at about the time to leave work, I felt as though I had learned nothing and was going to keep going in my ways. History repeats itself.

"Ali," Don said "Do you want to come over to my house tonight?" He knew I loved his family, especially Anthony. Usually being invited would be a joy for me, but I had nothing more to gain because I felt good already after talking with Don.

"No, I don't think do." I said, still with little confidence.

"Ali, you're coming over tonight!" he then ordered.

"Okay," I said. The drive over to his house was a blur to me. I didn't know what world I was in. I got to his house; his whole family was there. The members of the family were caught unexpected.

"Come here, sit down," his father said. I sat down. There was a short silence. I hate silences, I always feel that people think I'm crazy when there are silences. I saw an uneasy look on Don's face, I knew things would go down, because me going to their house is very unusual.

"This guy," I said to his dad, "Look at this guy, jeese!" when all he was doing was sitting down comfortably, something that I could not do. "Ha, ha, ha" we both laughed, knowing the situation. "You guys are the toughest family ever!" They all but one, Don, laughed hysterically, "We moved from San Francisco because of you." I felt like God. Every situation I'm in, I have to be in control. "You're gay?" I asked, he nodded yes and I said, "You might as well fuck me." He did.

What does this all mean? This thought popped up in my mind. *There has to be some reason to this insanity. Where is this all going?* Nowhere. I wasn't helping the world out in any way. Perhaps I created some love, and a few good laughs. *Why am I doing this?* I looked up at Anthony. I wanted to be him.

"Why are you here?" he said.

It all comes down to this question. I didn't know what he was talking about. My brain is like a wall; nothing can come through, no matter how relevant the message. "Why are you here?" he said again.

"There's nothing else to do!" I responded.

"I love you," he said. "Ali, I'm gay." I was so afraid of being thought of as gay. How would someone as confident as him say he's gay? "Ali, you're savior of the human race." I was a little more than gay. "Kill yourself." He kept repeating himself, "Kill yourself." I would just laugh.

"I have a gun, I'll kill you right now!" Don said.

"You're gay!" is all I responded.

"Here, I'll go get the gun."

"No, not yet" I said, "I'll kill myself later."

"Ali don't kill yourself, I'll kill myself," Anthony said. The whole family but Don would kill themselves if I died. Anthony knew my imbalance well, he knew who I was very well, "I love you." I was sure if he were given the same capabilities as I had he would act upon them.

"You might as well fuck me." He did and loved it.

"Ali, let me fuck you," his youngest brother Lenny said.

"No, you're going to live." He was too young to be a victim.

"Ali, I'm going to kill myself." Don said.

I looked at his dad and said, "How could you let your son kill himself?"

"If he wants to kill himself, it's his decision."

"No, trust me, I'll kill myself later." I had to keep in the back of my mind just to do it when the time comes, "do it" meaning kill myself—if I wouldn't, it would be a disaster. "Look at Anthony, he never asks the questions as to why we are here?"

"Anthony is a special person," Don said.

I looked at Lenny, "Lenny's shit." He wasn't as mentally gifted as the rest of the family.

"Lenny is shit, but he likes himself," said Don.

"What's Lenny going to do?" career-wise I meant.

"I love you," Anthony said. We are supposed to be happy, life is not about who can out-perform whom, it is about comradery. Most people are easy going with whatever they do, relying only on being happy.

"We might as well be together," I said.

"We'll take you," said Don. After all the hate he had towards me, he would still take me as a brother. That is how unusual I am. This was too big of a commitment. I remember as a kid sometimes trying to kill someone and later going to their house to be with them forever. My parents would always come and pick me up. I had to stay with my parents. It kept in check my plan to ruin the world. I left Don's house with that same blank and powerful feeling, with still no change in intelligence. I was in love with confusion.

Chapter 8

I was working at Lisa's and my big nose started to really bug me. I thought that was the reason why I didn't get girls. So, I knew I would have to get a nose job. Through an exhaustive search I found the best and brightest surgeon around. I made two or three visits with the doctor, all of which were straight-forward. He told me about the procedure and how it was going to cost $7000. I never said a word to him; I couldn't even look him in the eye. I knew whatever I would say would be stupid, so I shut up. I worked 6 months straight at Lisa's in order to pay the $7,000 for the operation.

The good times were rolling. I had some fun moments during that time period. I remember making all of the male workers depressed, always in a serious mood. All the female workers liked me, I rarely spoke to them and they did not find me annoying. If I were to talk to a girl the way I would talk to a guy back then, I would have just thought, *how could someone be so crazy?* Everything I said made no sense. For me, these were some of the best times in my life; for everyone else; the moment in their life when they were unhappiest.

The workers would tell me everything from, "You might as well come out of the closet," to a girl saying, "I have friends that will go out with Ali." At work, the night before my nose job, "Things are going to change!" my friend Ron said. "Nothing is going to change!" was his next comment. I knew my future would be interesting. On the outside I would change, I however, I would always be insane. This would be a pivotal movement of my life.

My mom drove me to the hospital at 6:00 in the morning. The doctor merely greeted me, and briefly told me how the procedure would be. The operation began. I was kind of nervous being operated on. I awakened, after begin unconscious for a period of two hours. "I'm going to U.S.C." I said shyly, I wanted to get his respect.

"What's your major?" he said.

"Business," *whoa, I talked to him; this guy is an amazing person and I talked to him.* I knew he was rich and smart, a combination I love. The surgery went on without any complications. It was almost finished.

"Almost done." he said.

"Take your time," I said.

He had a bewildered look on his face, but went on. "Okay finished."

I had to say something; I mean the guy just gave me surgery and I basically said nothing to him. "Did you get the tip?" He nodded yes, and began to talk.

Not letting him speak, I said, "Is it thinner?" He nodded yes again, and I quickly walked away from the doctor. I viewed the situation as one in which by letting him talk he would be better than me. I was having control. I was at the waiting room, and sat with my mom for a few seconds, while viewing the doctor.

"I can never love again," he said while shaking his head in sorrow. At the time I did not know why, so I just laughed. "Why are you doing this?" he said.

"There's nothing else to do," was my response. He didn't know what to say next after I said that. I saw a laugh forming, and it was at about the same level as I was. He had a look of a nervous breakdown. "You're gay!" I said. He was now property of Ali Mazhin. He now laughed like me and was over the fact that he could never love again, but was now in the realm of my world. He was married and had two kids. "Yeah, when you were younger, you and your friends sucked each other's dicks probably just three or four times."

"How do you know this?" he laughed.

"You're the best surgeon in the world!" I said. He was brought to emptiness; he was seeing existence just as I viewed it. We saw love in its strangest form. I felt I was better than him. "You're shit." I said hesitantly.

"I am not shit, I am John Baker, board certified plastic surgeon!" he said with amazement.

He laughed in astonishment, "How stupid are you?"

I could tell he'd never talked in the tone of voice that he did because it was crazy. I was just trying to keep our experience going. "I'm smart, I'm going to U.S.C."

"How did you get in? I'd think they'd have some sort of barriers to keep people like you out!"

I then said, "I'm smart, listen, people like watching basketball games with commercials, so they get the at-the-game feeling." It was a mind-bending statement that left me exhausted. I felt like Einstein.

"You just said you love me!" he said with strange body form.

"What are you thinking?" I asked.

"I'm thinking about the nose, and my wife…"

"Jeese both at the same time?"

"Yes" he said laughing.

"Say it then." I did not believe him. He used some medical jargon, I can't remember, but it was something like, "Is the anesthesia in the nose going to heal correctly?" All this without any real thought. My mind couldn't even come close to grasping it. "Jeese, you're so bad-ass, you might as well fuck me." We went in a room away from my mom and sex took place.

"What kind of car do you drive?" I asked.

"A Rolls Royce."

"Where do you live?" I asked.

"In Brentwood."

"Oh my god!" I said, loving the guy.

With the lunacy he said, "These are the thoughts you think, and regard as unimportant, all this stuff doesn't matter."

"Yes, it does, it's the most important thing, and you're the best person with it. We might as well be together." I said.

"I'll leave my wife and kids right now for good and be with you. I love you."

"Your wife?" I replied, "No, I bet she's hot, keep her, we'll fuck! You have kids?" I asked.

"Yeah, two boys." He replied.

"Whoa, I bet they're both bad-ass too!"

He was experiencing psychosis. "How did you make it this far?" he said in amazement. "Why are you doing this?" he repeated.

"There's nothing else to do!" I said again in a serious tone. The man seemed as though he was as high as I was. It was now to the point of wonder." "I'm going to be in a mental institution, come visit me." I said.

"No, I won't visit you," he said.

"Why not?? Ohh, it's because you're so bad-ass!
Oh my God." I said. "I'm going to kill myself."

He said, "No, don't kill yourself."

I said, "Then kill yourself."

He said, "I will later, then come to my funeral."

I said, "Okay, I will come to your funeral, but if you don't kill yourself, I'll kill myself." There was an attractive young receptionist who made appointments for the surgeon. She was still in the real world. "Look, you think she's hot," I said to him, "and you have an attraction towards him!" I said to the girl.

They looked at each other and gave a look like, "I guess you're right, but a relationship in reality would be out of the question."

It would be crazy. "Have sex with each other!" I commanded.

This is how life would be lived if people were like me. They did, right in front of me, my mom, and two other anesthesiologists. It seemed as though they did not know what they were doing but they loved it. "Put yourself in a mental institution right now," a lady said.

"Whoa, this lady is the best anesthesiologist! We might as well be together forever," I told her.

She did not buy it. "Check yourself in to a hospital right now."

I didn't think there was anything wrong with me. I just wanted to be, as I wanted them to be. "No, I'll be with John." Then John came towards me and he stood next to her waiting for what I'd say next.

I knew my mom was thinking there was a chance I would elope with the doctor. I would have everything I ever dreamed of---money, a wife (John's), and brothers to play with. I was nearing the end of my life and this would make me win both ways. One, I would have my track record, and two, I would not kill myself and would be rich without any work, laughing at the world. Or I could go with my mom, go through another two years of being stupid, and finally find out who I am. "Mom, let's go."

"Cancel all my appointments for two weeks," John said with rage. "I'm going to see my wife right now."

I left the office with a despondent mother, and walked with her to the car. My body was experiencing euphoria, I felt alive. I quickly forgot everything that had happened. A splint had been out on my nose near the end of the surgery, and I would have to go back the next week to get it taken off. I was really nervous that whole week and I didn't know why.

I came into the office; I made no eye contact with John, the receptionist smiled at me. John took the splint off, as if nothing had ever happened. I would eventually remember the scene, and from what I hear he does not remember the scene, and from what I hear he does not remember me. As I am today, the incident was a delusion? How can it feel so real? Are these experiences so insane that sometimes the person I'm affecting also forgets? The mind is huge, and capable of anything.

I still sometimes kick myself for not staying with him. The rock band, "Faith no More," made a song that fits into this situation, it sang, "You want it all but you can't have it, it's in your face but you can't grab it. What is it? It's it. What is it? It's it." The end of the music video featured a fish out of water grasping for life. Nothing made me happy.

I have gone through so many sets of friends it's amazing. With each set, I'd go through the same silliness and confusion as the last. It is better to call them sufferers than friends because each person's happiness decreases by knowing me. That is probably true about a lot of people, but my experiences were different. Most of the times when I would be cruel to my friends, they would not say anything back to me.

I was always interested in control, and power. I always talked; I loved every one of my friends. On the outside I may appear gay, but once someone knows me they think otherwise. Still, today most of the people I know think I'm gay. This does not bother me, it does not matter what other people think, all that matters are what you think.

To really get into it, I probably would enjoy the first couple of weeks of being gay, but I think more about it, and see nothing in my head, and that's when earthquakes, and thunder occur. I am left with nothing. I do not know what could be scarier than a person's fear of causing a natural disaster. My fear of fear is great. If I were to let all my thoughts roll, I would be an extremely dangerous blank entity that causes destruction and fear to the hearts of many. So, when instances come down to actual sexuality, I would naturally distance myself from the person. As close as I could become to someone, I was just not there.

One time the truth all came out. The usual Friday night at the age of 18 would consist of drinking beers, and talking about life. This night most of my close friends were there. I was a pilot in the airplane controlling the situation. Everything I would say either meant, "I love you" or "I hate you." There was no middle ground. No one had the balls to stand up to me. I would just keep yapping of how I was better than everyone else, and what low sources of life gays are.

One night a friend started to like me, as I liked him. It was okay for a little bit, but he kept talking for about a minute, and I felt like we were connecting, and close. *Disgusting*, I thought, *a man and a man actually being sexually interested in each other*. I completely stopped talking to him or laughing at his jokes for a few minutes, I was in disgust.

"Oh, I see, I see how it is," my friend Stan said, referring to how I could like him, but he can't like me back. He then questioned his already preconceived opinion on whether or not I was gay "Who are you?" he asked with forcefulness and meaning.

I felt out of the closet, my friends knew me too well, so I could not let what he said be forgotten. Everyone was curious. “I’m a pimp!” I said, this was the first thing that came to my mind.

“You’re a pimp! What? Ha, ha, ha.”

I got off my chair and walked to the kitchen table, standing there thinking with joy. “What am I?” I asked.

“Ali, you’re crazy!” said Jim.

I shrugged off what he said and wanted to hear more. I knew this would be a significant moment in my life. “I’m not a person.” I said in confusion.

“You are a person,” Jim said, “You’re crazy.”

I acted clueless and wanted to know what other people thought of me. My presence was somewhat supernatural. “You’re evil!” Ron said.

“Ali, you’re gay, I’m gay,” Stan said. “You love people, Ali, you love me. It seems like you either love me or hate me. Come out of the closet.”

I looked at Jim, “Ali, you’re crazy!” Jim said again. Worlds were colliding in my head. At one moment I thought I was a normal person, other times evil, and sometimes crazy. I felt like I was in control of the whole world.

“Ali, I’d take advantage of your powers and have fun for a few days. Go out and take whatever you want from a store, or have sex with a hot girl, Then kill yourself. Ali, what are you doing? Said Stan.

“No, because then my Grand Plan would go to waste.” As stupid as I was I still knew what I was doing. “No, I’m gay!” I said, wanting for it to be a simple, clear-cut problem that I could fix easily, and realize that I’m like other people. I just had to come out of the closet.

“You’re not gay,” Jim said.

Damn, I thought, I knew it all along. I knew if I came out of the closet I was in, then I’d be known as a crazy person, and life would be tedious and monotonous. I was coming to terms with the truth. With all the energy and attention in the room focused on me, I became mentally high and happy, just as with the crazy sex. It was a feeling that most people can never achieve. I felt like Satan at that moment, where everything I’d say would be sacred. “I feel like a

God whose presence wants to be felt, and I can set people straight," I said.

"It's like you're part God and part devil," Stan said.

"You're evil," Ron said again.

I was scared to think this was true because nothing would be worse than being labeled evil and uncontrollable. However, the next thing Jim said was, "They thought you were evil, for a long time." I was listening, and he then flat out said with confidence, "You're not evil."

"Look at Jim, he is going to become President of the United States!"

"Jim?" I looked in astonishment.

"Ali, they're going to make me president. I've saved so many lives." I did not care, however, because he was my best friend, and I would never look at him as anyone else but that.

"Jim, did you…"

"Yeah, did you…"

"Yeah."

Jim was the only person who truly knew who I was and we got along like no two others could. "Ali, nobody likes you." They all deeply loved me, but on a sane personal level I didn't allow myself to be liked. "Kill yourself."

"I'll kill myself later, it's part of the plan, I have to do well at U.S.C.," I said.

"Why are you going there? I don't know what I'm going to do with my life."

I'm going there because I love Chip." He was a good friend who was living his life the way I thought it should be lived. "I'm going to kill myself."

"You're not going to kill yourself," said Jim.

"I'm going to kill myself," I said again with confidence.

"Ali, there will be a day when there is a slight chance you will kill yourself, but you're not going to do it." Jim said.

"I'm going to kill myself," I again said with meaning.

"That's another thing Ali, don't kill yourself." Jim meant this, the world would be in chaos, and there would be a long recovery time after my death.

"I'm not going to remember this." I said. I was much too high.

"Ali, if you remember anything, it's that you can't kill yourself; you'll try to plenty of times and it's not going to work," said Jim.

"What about earthquakes?" I was curious to know if I caused them.

"They think you do." said Jim.

"Ali, I love you," my Australian friend named Chip said. "Everything you say. I just have to laugh. Sometimes I don't know how you make it to this house to hang out! Sometimes I just wanted to sock you in the face for the things you say." He then went on to say that everything negative I say is always on the tip of his mind but he restrains himself from saying it because it's too mean. "Ali, I'm smart," he then said.

"What, you're smart?" I thought he was average.

"Ali, they moved me from Australia because they knew you would like me, I have saved so many lives I have been close to moving to the Midwest to get away from you several times." He would live a much more sensible and happy life there.

Stan then said, "What is so bad about being gay?"

I replied, All you do is sit at home depressed, and think about how bad life is!"

"No, I'm happy," he laughed. "What do you think life is, just drink and talk non-stop! No, we enjoy other people's company, we don't hate." He said laughing, "I've sucked Jim's dick, just to know that this is the President of the United States!"

"Jim?" I said with curiosity.

"Ali, I have nothing else to do, the nights you don't hang out, I hang out with them.

"Yeah, we are the champions, gay people are the best people. I want to suck Chips dick."

"If you want to," he said.

"You're gay!"

"I'm not gay," he said seriously.

"You're shit!" I said.

"I'm not shit," he said. I now felt bad. "Ali, I love you, don't kill yourself, I'll then kill myself," he said tearfully.

"What if they put me in a coma or something?"

"Ali without you here…" he couldn't finish, I understood.

"But why, why do I always ask myself that question?"

"Ali we all get that," Stan said.

"Jim doesn't!" Jim laughed. "Jim is a special person." "Do you?" I asked, referring to confusing questioning of existence.

He admitted, "I do."

"Jim is the best all-around character you could be. He's perfect, just look at him."

"Ali, I can never love anyone as much as you."

"Jim's gay!" I said.

"I'm not gay," he replied in all honesty. "Ali, you've made me think I'm gay." A pause, he was going somewhere, "You've made me hate gay people." He said as I laughed, "Ali you've made me think I'm crazy." I laughed harder. I knew that I could drain people of their sanity, even the most special of people, but even Jim? "Ali, I think you're crazy," Jim said, giving me his diagnosis. I then slowly sat next to Jim because he knew the most truth about me.

"You're savior of the human race!" a Persian coworker said with anger.

I looked at Jim, "That's the only thing we don't know," by "we" referring to many expert opinions rolled into one.

"Ali, there have always been crazy people, you just never hear about them." I guess this is because if we give them fame, then we as a society fail. Crazy people should not be regarded as special; the real special people are the well-educated, and interesting people who benefit society. "Ali, there are people even crazier than you!" Jim said.

"No!" I'm not the craziest." I wanted to be the most core human being to ever live. "How many are there?" I asked.

"There's like a thousand."

"Why don't they all just kill themselves?" I said.

"Ali, kill yourself!" said Stan.

After some silence, Jim continued, "Ali, you've caused so many people to hate themselves."

"What is after I'm better (an adult) I reverse everything bad I did and get people's lives normal?"

"You're too stupid," said Jim.

"No, I'm smart." *Am I smart?* I thought.

"You're the dumbest guy in the world, you're as dumb as a fish. Ali, I'm so smart, I am one of the smartest people in the world. I'm the smartest guy in Detroit. The whole city was given tests to see who would deal with you best. I had to pass so many tests."

"What are you thinking?" I said.

"Did my mom let the cat out today?"

"Who cares!" I said.

Jim proceeded, "Ali, there are some people that look over your life who are so smart they make me look dumb. Ali, there are whole regions of the country that don't know about you. You cannot get to them no matter how much destruction you end up doing. Ali, there are some people so smart that they don't even know about you."

If I had killed myself that day with that slight chance, a shock wave of pure power would be given off. The power would initially say, "Kill yourself, I did and you love me." It would have gone through states and everyone would feel my final wrath and die with me.

"You're going to have an accounting teacher at U.S.C. that you're going to love. He'll be Indian. You'll also have a girlfriend, she'll be Latin, because I like Latin's!" I felt hope, because I would actually have a girlfriend. "Nothing makes you happy," Jim then said, implying a chemical imbalance in my brain.

"We can't kill you. They have even thought of dropping an atomic bomb on the whole city just to kill you."

"No, they can't do that!" I said. As cold-hearted an idea as it was, it would have been the best option when I was very young. "Am I ever on the News?"

"Sometimes, because they know you never watch it." Said Jim. *What does it all mean, where do I fit in with the theories of life?*

"But survival of the Fittest, it's not true," I pleaded.

"Ali, some of the brightest people in the world went over and over it to check out its validity. They even tool some of Mr. Darwin's theory out, the theory is true."

The findings were true, the theory is correct. I am the least fit person in the world. I am meant to look absolutely useless if I act out my thoughts. I am meant to be homeless. However, I am still alive and not homeless. I guess I am the loophole in the theory.

"I'm fit," Jim said.

"What is your future Jim?" I asked.

"I'll go to law school, join the army, I'll be governor and then president."

"But what if there is someone smarter and better than you for president?"

"Ali, they're just going to give it to me, I've saved so many lives, I'm like a God."

"Anything else?" I asked.

"They're building this machine to kill you." Jim said.

"What kind of machine, what will it do?"

"All you're going to have to do is step in."

"What if I cause an earthquake? What if my sheer energy will break it?"

"It will be earthquake proof, and you won't be able to break it. It will be everything-proof."

"But what if I'm better?" I asked that question as to when I'm an adult and I become a good person who no longer commits wrong, as I believe I am today. I wanted to know if I will still be sentenced to death if I'm completely rehabilitated.

"We need closure," Jim said.

Again, I repeated. "Even if I'm better?"

"We need closure," Jim said again.

"What if I don't step in?"

"Then it's either going to be you or me." It would be a disaster if I let Jim die.

"Jim," I said, "you kill me."

"They wouldn't make me president," he said.

What drama, I thought. "I'm going to change," I told everyone. "I have to see everything before I die," meaning by this, experiencing every situation and every reality that I possibly could.

Jim then said, "You're going to try to kill me, and.."

"What?" I thought, I could never dislike Jim. However, deep down inside I knew it was going to happen. On the tip of my tongue I wanted to tell him "I'm sorry," so I wouldn't have to say it later.

"You can't kill me," Jim said. "Ali, you're going to not even want to hang out with me anymore." He continued, "You're going to go to parties and just talk to girls. You're even going to say it's okay to be gay. You're going to try to kill everyone." A pause so Jim could collect his thoughts, "You're going to rule the world. You're going to write a book and become rich. You're going to get fat. You'll be in and out of institutions. You'll think you're gay."

What? I thought, *who am I if I'm not skinny?*

Jim proceeded, "You're going to love classical music." I love it with a passion. "They even named a street in California University (where Jim attends) with the word 'gay' in it so you'd find me when you mentally collapse."

I was thinking and said, "Jim, this is how it's going to end, I'm going to call Joe, and go to his house, and ask to suck his dick, then go to California University for the both of you to witness me kill myself."

"Oh no, Ali, don't ask to suck my dick. Don't kill yourself," Joe said.

"I'll eventually remember all of this and I'll kill myself." The energy in the air this whole time caused even my friends to be high, and not be able to remember everything.

"Ali, I won't have a gun." Jim said, but I thought there would still be one anyway. Now the feeling of sex was in the air, "Ali, can I fuck you?" Jim asked.

"Yeah," I said. I called him gay and shit, and he did not say a word. He knew me so well that he knew all I did in life was blabber nonsense, and I really did not mean anything. "Jim, one day after hanging out I dropped you off early, just so I could masturbate. I wanted to fuck you." I said.

"Ali, I'd let you."

"Can I fuck you?" I asked. I did, how many men can say they have fucked the President of the United States?

"Ali, sometimes I just wanted to rip down your pants and…" Jim said. I knew what he meant.

"Ali, can I fuck you?" Joe asked, as he asked me before at work.

"Yeah."

He did and said hysterically, "You're sooo stupid." We both laughed with joy. "What are you thinking?" he asked.

"Why would I say that, why would I do that, why..?!"

My relationship with Joe was basically the same type he had with his girlfriend. She showered him with her love and was like a slave. "Even my girlfriend says things during sex!"

"Jeese, like what?" I asked.

"Move to the side so I could get a better position!" *Wow*, I thought, *someone could think that way?* Chip had a girlfriend named Amy. She witnessed everything.

"Amy has sucked my dick," said Stan. "It is just something people do to show they like each other."

"Amy, suck my dick." I said. She did and during that time I said, "You like me?"

"You're funny," she said.

"We might as well have sex."

"I don't love you."

"Ohh, so you fuck only if you love, I see." This was all new to me. Someone actually liked me. The feeling of emptiness left. "Amy, you're shit." I needed to feel like the worse human ever to live.

She stopped pleasuring me and said, "I can't like you anymore."

"Why, Ohh because you like yourself."

"Ali can I fuck you?" My Mexican co-worker said. This was a co-worker that never got any love from me. He was gay and it was always ridiculous the way I spoke to him. It was like no love could be stronger, and he was unhappy most the time when I spoke to him. I knew he was gay. Sometimes, he even said in front of everyone, "Come on Ali, suck my dick." I always just laughed.

He began to speak, "Ali, I have AIDS."

"What? Why didn't you say anything?"

"Because of you!" he laughed.

He used a condom, and I yelled, "Take it off!"

"No," he laughed.

"No, take it off now, who cares."

"Ali, no" he said with laughter. He finished and said with his accent, "Youuu crazy!"

"Ha, ha, ha," we connected with madness. He was one of the hand-chosen people that I was certain to like.

I maintained the high for a few more days' controlling everyone at work. It was as if we were all in an insane asylum. "Everyone, just ask to suck my dick, because I never know when the right time is."

I hung out with Jim, as usual, and our usual conversations were taking place, and he said, "I don't know, do you want to suck my dick?"

"Yeah," I said.

"Right here?"

"Yeah." I did, and tried to like it but I was forcing myself. I didn't like it.

"Ali, you don't have to."

"Okay, I don't want to, I'll tell you when I want to." Minutes passed, I got in a better mood. "Now I want to!" I did, called him "gay," he laughed, it was just humor. Then the thought came, how I had to get everyone, even Jim, "You're shit!" I said.

He pulled his pants up and said, "Ali, you're crazy." The truth had been laid upon me.

I'm crazy, I thought, just as I thought when I was a little boy in the institution and worlds collided. *Nothing has changed. Why am I here? Why even live the rest of the day? No*, I thought to myself. I could see what was in my future, no more insane joy. I would not feel special. I must remain stupid. "Why do I say that?" I asked Jim.

"Ali, you're crazy." He said. So, I dropped him off at home and thought to myself, and tried to bring myself back to the way things were before, the fun insanity, without anything ever being sexual.

Another person I tried to kill was Rick. I worked with him at Lisa's. This was the same Rick who was, "the toughest guy in the world," that I had met earlier as a child in an institution. Years ago, he had even lived next-door to me, to be closer to me. He was a really good person. I always gave him respect because he was older. He and I played basketball with each other often after work. One day during a one-on-one game, pressure built up inside me, and I yelled, "Why am I here?"

"I don't know why you're here," he said.

"Did you…? I asked.

"I…," he responded.

"You might as well fuck me."

He did and said, "Don't talk to people," because I was so crazy. "Don't even look at people."

I can't even walk by someone without them questioning me. "I love you. Ali, I'm the toughest guy in the world, my brother and I moved from Michigan to live next door to you."

"Your brother?" I said, "Oh, yeah, now I remember seeing him at a garage sale you guys had, he is the most self-assured person ever. We might as well live together." I said.

"Ali, I'm gay." He said.

"No, you're not, you're too tough." Although work was little I was satisfied, "You're shit." He didn't say anything. What is it? "You're shit," I said again. I saw a hurt look in his eyes. Whatever I was saying affected him, I felt alive. "Yeah, you're shit, you're the worst person to ever live." It hurts writing this now, knowing that I said this, but I did. I then walked away from him, happy. He watched me walk off, in pain as if his mother had died. I quickly forgot.

I saw him the next day at work, and could tell he was hurt. I acted as though nothing has happened, because I had already repressed that fact that this event even took place. Don was there, he spoke, "Ali, what happened yesterday with Rick?" I had no answer, and tried to ignore him. I tried to go to the next subject. "He fucked you," Don continued. Rick took his pizza delivery and quickly left. "Say it Ali, he fucked you." I stood quietly, and laughed. "No, it's not funny, say it."

"He fucked me." I could barely say it and it hurt. I knew what had happened deep down inside, however, my interpretations of reality were so different from normal that it didn't really bother me.

Chapter 9

I was down to one of the last days of being completely ignorant as to what has gone on in my life. I saw the movie *Donnie Brasco.* Johnny Depp portrayed his character Donnie with brilliance. Donnie was someone I thought I could be, if only I thought about things a little while longer before saying them. He was like me, if I got my act together.

I was 19, getting ready to start U.S.C., and thought to myself, I must do this now. If that is who I am I must be that person. I must get ready to take on the world. I gave money to the cashier for a pizza I delivered. Instead of shaking like a nervous person, and being scared of how rational the person is compared to myself, I asked myself, *What would Donnie Brasco do?* I stood there like a mogul and felt the cashier give me respect. That's when I thought; *Wow I have it in me to be the best.*

I gradually stopped with the humor that no one else could do, because I thought Donnie wouldn't talk like that. I started renting other famous movies, *The Godfather* series, *Good Fellows*, *Lawrence of Arabia*, and *Scar Face.* I tried to mimic every important character in the movies. "Ali, what's going on? You used to be more animated." I was losing what little life I had. I thought, *that was the old Ali, I have to be serious* now. I stopped talking to all the guys at work and only talked to the girls.

"Ali, I'm impressed," my boss said as he saw me talking to a girl.

"Nothing is written," I said. I thought I was Lawrence of Arabia. I felt as though I was the greatest man to ever live, a legend or hero. He didn't understand what I meant by this line, but I loved it. I would tall any male employee who talked to me to, "Fuck off!" I asked a girl, who I had just met at work, for a date. She accepted and I would not say a word to her. She tried to keep a conversation going, but I was just not there. It became scary how weird I acted towards her.

My friends started to know I was changing, and asked me, "Are you okay?" I went to work some days and did not talk to anyone. That is what Al Pacino would do. So of course, I was okay "Ali's, been in a bad mood, it's rubbed off on me, Ali has that effect on people."

A chef said, "Ali's crazy," a co-worker told me.

The dishwasher would imitate pointing a gun to my face with his hand and pull the trigger. "Bam," he said. *If only someone can pull the trigger.* I still had the power of their love, because there were still bonds of friendship. However, after a while I broke every friendship to the point of nothingness. I gave the cold shoulder to all of my close friends. I recall one friend almost crying, while pulling his hair. *I'm the Godfather why would I care?*

I started to think, *wait, if I can shower guys with love I can also shower girls.* I started to only think about girls, everything else was gay. I only wanted to hang out with straight people. My gay co-worker also started to mimic me with attitude, by not talking to anyone and talking to the girls. "Ali, look at what you are doing to me!" he said in agony. I walked away as though I was God.

I started making new friends, in different manners. I started to like people, not love people, and I tried never to do anything gay. Only objective statements would now come out of my mouth—nothing queer. Today this has stuck with me; I can no longer come up with queer statements. I wish I could so I could give some examples in this book for you to read and laugh at. I can no longer come up with the insane humor, which left me—all the super life left me. I can no longer get into close personal relationships either. It is too scary, and it sickens me.

The friendship I regret ending most was Jim's. He was the closet I have ever been to someone, and vice versa. We were probably the closet two people in history. It took a long time to kill that friendship, a lot of misery that we both went through. Everything I said was unlike me. He didn't know who I was anymore. I treated him as if I was constantly pointing a gun to his head. It got to the point where he knew that I was trying to "kill" him.

We made a trip to Santa Barbara to visit a friend. He forgot directions to our friends house. "I'm so pissed!" he yelled like I've never seen him yell, "I can't believe I can't find it. I'm so pissed!" This is as low as he could get. If I had given him a gun, he'd probably be dead.

I should have been happy, but I said, "Jim, it's not a test."

He kept wondering what the hell I was going through. What the hell did I want? Was I depressed? "Ali you don't have to drink if you don't want to."

"I know." He out in a pornographic video; we watched it and drank in misery.

"Ali, what is it?" he finally said.

"It's nothing." I replied. I made the friendship so that we could not experience any harmony. In Santa Barbara I would walk by cars and hit the mirrors off with my fists. I would talk to police officers with no respect. I thought that I was smarter than doctors. I didn't socialize with anyone, but I tried very hard to maintain an image that I was better than everyone.

One night at a friend's house, my friends and I got drunk and hungry. "Let's make pasta, do you know how to make it?" someone said.

"I don't know anything." Doctors sometime say the same thing. The truth is, no one really, "knows" anything. Language and thought is all subjective.

"What do you mean? "asked my friend I shrugged him off as stupid. Everything I said was "real." In order for me to talk, conversation had to do with girls or something really happening. I would interoperate an event so that I would feel nothing out of it. I didn't want to feel pressure. I was heading towards a nervous breakdown.

Jim and I were talking about the stock market, and whether to put money in it. "I wouldn't be putting anything to put money in it. "I wouldn't be putting anything in it now," he said. He thought I'd actually get so low and kill myself, the market would crash, and he'd lose most of his money. Slowly in time, I knew what I was doing to him and tried to reverse it. Every night we hung out was like a test to me to see how well I could act.

We were playing pool, "I'm never going to drink again as soon as I start U.S.C."

"Ali, U.S.C. is making you crazy." Jim was to go off to school. The night before he left, it finally felt like old times. We were laughing like the good old days. I looked over to him and saw a tear in his eyes. I really meant a lot to him. I continued to hang out with him at his school every now and then. After I caused all the damage I could, I quit Lisa's. I had to aim higher and ruin the world; I had a lot more people to inflict my pain upon.

I started U.S.C. and tried real hard to be studious. I wanted to graduate. I had some of my smartest people in the world teaching me. My early prophecies from being in the world institutionalized as a child turned out to be true. My Communications teacher was the smartest woman in the world, who I met when I was young and in an institution. She was there to help me finish my game. I became so stressed in class; trying to act normal, that it hurt my head. I would raise my eyebrows in fear, trying to blend in with the rest if the kids. The teacher once saw this and turned around in fear.

We had various exercise's in class. The first was to introduce your classmate to the class. I introduced my friend properly, and when she introduced me I was in a blank. I did not know how to act, feel, or stand. The whole class was looking at me. My eyes wandered from side to side at a rapid speed. This was an "out of the closet" crazy experience. Within minutes everyone knew who I was. One person even laughed. This is no surprise; I get laughed at least three times a day. I have had homeless people laugh at me.

When she finished introducing me I was relieved, *Phew*, I thought, *I hope I don't have to go through that again*. The next exercise was one where the teacher put five people in a circle; we were all to rotate and look at the class. "Watch them, maintain eye contact with them," the teacher said. I was starting to get the same feeling of not knowing what to do. I didn't know if I could handle a few more seconds of this. As I was turning with the other students the teacher said, "See who they are." With the worst timing too, my eyes were in the side of my head.

"Oh my god," I heard. Was the teacher doing this on purpose? I think she wanted to let me know that I couldn't hide forever. I must accept who I am. She videotaped various speeches by students and talked about the flaws of their speeches to the class.

Everyone had something wrong; when she got to me however, she was saying things I just could not understand. It was like a different language, but one line will stick with me forever, "We're meant to be happy." I think of this all the time. How is it I can't be happy? "Beautiful smile," she said.

After about a month or two, the stress of both school and finding out "who I was" became too great a task for me to handle. I entered a mental institution; I had not even made it to my first midterm. I spent a few weeks in the institution, going through complete psychosis. I was as crazy as can be. I was unlike anyone. Fear took the driver's seat. Enormous amounts of love and hate were distributing everywhere.

One can only be down so long. As the weeks passed it all started to fade away, and I had to go back to my "real" life. I felt I was ready to give school another chance. I was still stupid. Self-actualization was not complete. Coming out, I was given royal treatment; everyone was amazingly nice to me. In my Communications class I gave a speech about business ethics. I started talking about the subject, but I wasn't there actually telling the facts. What did it all mean? There was something that I wanted even more than an A on my presentation: a human life.

As I started talking, I unexpectedly heard laughter in the back of the room, two students were gesturing to each other about my speech. I then saw the teacher put her head down and laugh to herself. She could not hold her head up to listen to me. I spoke in a tone too powerful for her to listen to. With anger I spoke in a tone to make it look like I was master of puppets. The speech wasn't about informing, it was about conforming. Having others to conform to my thoughts. "Look, he's trying to kill the teacher!" I heard. She sat shaking her head and tried desperately to look up while I spoke but she couldn't do it. The whole class was under my spell.

After it was through, she asked to speak with me in private, just as I told her to as a child. We would then be together. Subconsciously I thought that this would happen. I was scared as to what she would say to me when I saw her. At the time I felt the whole world was waiting around in fear to see what I was going to do next in my life. I chickened out. I asked a classmate, "When's the teacher supposed to get here?"

"Oh, she's coming right now," she said as if she knew my situation. I had never even met her, but she urged me to wait. I could not stand still due to my mental health. I left, and the teacher persisted in trying to talk to me three more times, as she called my house. (I would like to speak to her today, so if you're reading, give me a call.)

In my Organizational Behavior class, the teacher named Kenneth ended up being the same person who had told me my reason for being on Earth was to control the population. He would teach class without using notes. He would just talk from the knowledge off the top of his head. Two hours of brilliant nonstop lecturing. He began to tell the class about his personal profile. He attended Cornell University, and graduated top of his class. He worked for Procter and Gamble for ten years. Then he wrote many books about the science of Organizational Behavior. He lived in a rich part of Palos Verdes. I thought nothing of him at the time. I didn't think that I had anything to do with the man, but I did. He made all these accomplishments for me.

The two classes I spoke of above have little if any meaning, as does the next teacher. During the beginning of the semester when I registered for classes, I found a perfect schedule. No breaks in between classes, and all at my desired times. Next I received a phone call from the school, "Sorry, your Accounting class is cancelled due to low enrollment. We will automatically enroll you in the Tuesday-Thursday class from 4-6 p.m." I was upset. I tried to set my schedule up many ways in order to avoid the class, but I couldn't. The teacher turned out to be Indian. He had a full-face beard and was young, about 40. He kind of looked like an Indian Jim Morrison (with beard). He had a very serious face, and expressed no emotion. It seemed as though he was in touch with reality that I think is the truth, hence the best. After two or three sessions of busy work in order to see how well we knew the material, he introduced himself, "My first name is Habib, and I studied the theory of Natural Selection, as an undergraduate at Dartmouth. I primarily dealt with the Survival of the Fittest theory, which I don't believe in."

Wow, I thought. I hated that theory, because I was not fit. I wanted to believe it was not true, so my actions were justified. I initially had a liking for the teacher. On the outside, however, my mind was blank. I had no idea who this guy really was, and I had no idea as to what the future would hold in this class. He continued, "I got my M.B.A. in Accounting at Harvard Business School." He said Harvard with authority, making the class know through the Dean of U.S.C., whom I met at Harvard while still in school." The dean was the smartest man in the world, named Frank, who I spoke of earlier. I had U.S.C. under total control. The dean and the teachers were all puppets set up by me.

"I worked as a financial banker for five years and controlled millions of dollars in assets." He basically said he was rich. "I then went back to my village in India, where I built a church." He was a god. In the back of my head I knew him. It was Habib, who had earlier told me he was evil. I felt like we knew each other. However, there was still plenty of pieces missing.

In subsequent classes he said that in order to get a good grade in the class, you must read the material over five times. He stressed five times because this is how I got into U.S.C. by going over something so many times that it sticks in your short term memory. With the teacher giving the class the idea, I felt like a smart person. A true smart person only needs to read something one or two times and all is understood. They are bright and everything comes easier to them. They see things in black and white. There is always a clear-cut solution. I am not always bright. Slowly I started to feel more and more of a bond with him. *This guy is like me*, I thought.

He was talking and said, “Do your homework next time while drinking a glass of brandy.” The whole class laughed. We all loved the idea of drinking and studying. I especially loved the sound of the word, “Brandy.” It is high class and fun, and the teacher said he drank it sometimes while studying. I was now a happy student. The teacher sometimes came in and out of class with a can of Diet Coke, my favorite. This time in the middle of discussion, and out of nowhere he said, “Students, study tonight with some brandy.” Some students laughed, but I laughed a little harder. One more time later in the semester, he used the word, “brandy,” this time I was the only person in the class who laughed, it was as if he were talking only to me. The comment flew by everyone but my head. It was strange. The word brandy was now subconsciously stuck in the back of my head; however, I would not know it for months.

The teacher used PowerPoint to teach the class, he would just read off the screen. On some slides were pictures to help represent accounting facts. With a straight face he said, “This time we will use fish to demonstrate the process.” Everyone laughed. I gave a fake laugh, but I did not know what was so funny. He went on in a serious tone, “The fish are caught by fisherman who are represented in the equation.” Again, everyone laughed, and I gave a fake laugh. The teacher was quiet.

“What’s so funny?” the girl who sat next to me said. She knew I was being made fun of but acted dumb. She wanted to let me know that I was not alone in not getting the joke. “The fish caught by the fisherman are then fished out as you do in the equation.” Harder laughter came out; this time I didn't laugh. I was a little afraid. *Why are they laughing?*

"He's so awesome," I heard in the back. The teacher had somehow put both the words "brandy" and "fish" in the back of my head, and class resumed. I sat through it not understanding anything. I later lost what little concentration I had towards my studies and in a few days I would use hat little sanity I had and enter a mental institution.

Chapter 10

It all started. I was becoming clueless as I'd ever been. I questioned people about things that I kept bottled inside of me, as if it were my last day on earth. "Mom, I'm not like the son that you thought you would have." I thought that my mom was upset, deep inside, about how she raised me.

She then gave me a reaction like, "You're my son and I will always love you."

Another day went by and I came home crying to my mother, "Mom, I'm gay. Mom, I'm sorry, I'm gay." I said while hugging her, "Mom, I love people. Mom, my friend said that he could never love someone as much as he did me." She held me while listening. "Mom, he said he could never love again, Mom, I'm gay." I spoke like it was a tragedy. I spoke like I was on my deathbed. *Okay*, I thought, *I'm gay, I'll deal with it. Things should be okay.*

The next day came a midterm in my Organizational Behavior class. "Have you studied for the midterm?" I asked a lady friend.

"No, why would I care?"

I just laughed. I liked her. I got her to be in the same level as me. I inflicted my pain upon her. It made me happy.

My next class was Statistics. The class was a small one, with fifteen or twenty people. The atmosphere was relaxed. All of a sudden, I began laughing, with no control. I tried my hardest to stop, but I couldn't for about thirty minutes. The other people in the class would turn around and give me a strange glare. At the time I didn't know why I was laughing, but subconsciously I was thinking of all the insane deeds I had committed. I was indeed insane, with no sense of reality. This was my evil soul emerging. Deep down inside I felt bad. I knew the students were questioning why I was in class.

More time passed and I was slowly grounded. My first midterm was tomorrow. I had to study. I began to read my book in order to get well-prepared. I began to read in order to get well-prepared. Five minutes passed and I was realizing I was nuts. I could mentally read the words on the page, but I could not process them. If I were to recite the words to someone it would have been as if I was talking to a wall. It was just words. *I'm not gay, I'm crazy*. Everything came crashing down. I was a blank spirit. There was nothing real about me. I was just a human body with no purpose for being there. Why would I study for the midterm?

The paranoid thoughts I kept repressed throughout the years backlashed like a bullet. I could no longer separate my thoughts. I was held hostage by the truth. The reality I was hiding from everyone came into my life. I was crazy, and could not go on with the charade any longer.

I went to my sister's room with fear. "Maryam, I'm crazy." She said nothing and listened. She was not prepared for this. I repeated myself, and gave myself no opportunity for hope. Nothing anyone could say would change my opinion. This was the most solid thought that I had ever had. "I'm going to call a psychologist."

"No, then…" I paused and thought of how things should work out in my "Grand Plan." I started to remember all my old friends, and how I thought they were trained to be my friends. The world was a big stage and I was the main actor that must be kept alive. Everything that was ever said to me was rehearsed in order to avoid chaos if I died. I thought of how people thought I was funny, because I was crazy, and it made me laugh. It was all a bog joke. I thought of the tests people had to pass in order to know me. I thought of the degree of love that I can give relative to others. I remembered my early years and the trauma I was supposed to.

"We're the smartest people in the world," is what I remember most people saying to me. My delusion of grandeur was like no one else's. My sexual experiences kept popping up. One by one, I was remembering every person that I had known. My sexuality came out. I was neither gay, nor straight, but crazy—thriving on madness.

One of my sister's friends came over, and I mentally tried my hardest to get into her pants. I was producing an unbelievable amount of love. I tried harder than any human can try, but just couldn't get her to get with me. She truly was special. There are some people that I just cannot affect. "Let's go to Bryan house," she said. The look in her eye was saying, "You can't play with me, you're insane."

The two left for a couple of hours and when they returned I was still in the exact position on my sister's bed as when they had left. I just lay there with no feeling. I thought my time was up. The games I played, although fun, had no significance. My reason for being here arrived, no reason. I felt the world on my shoulders. I analyzed myself, for what I thought was logical. I now cared what others thought about me. I was slowly losing the power of having the who the "real" Ali Mazhin was. People would now slowly lose their love for me. Perhaps they would not want to kill themselves anymore if I died.

I felt bad and wanted to stop the insanity. I had to stop forcing all of my energy away from me, and started to focus on myself, to accept reality. My sister left home to go to work and she said, "Don't do anything stupid." I went to my room and called about seven or eight people who I cared about and spoke in a completely different language that they were used to hearing from me.

I had to think of greatness. *Who is the best person I know?* I spoke to Joe who was from "the best family in the world." It was unexpected because I never call him. "What are you doing now, Joe?"

"Nothing," he said strangely. I could tell he was startled when I called.

"I'm coming over right now." I said with confidence.

"Okay," he said unsurely. I wanted to say goodbye to the world. It's been fun but the show's over. As I drove over I saw a few people waving their hands good bye to me.

One person said, "Good bye" while laughing. I saw a friend from work on the way and instead of waving my usual hello; I circled my finger and pointed it to my head. My friends laughed with the gesture. However, I felt my time was up. I knew it and everybody else knew it. I had to kill myself that day. It would do society a great favor.

After the third time driving past his house, I recognized it. Joe came out and greeted me kindly. We looked at the view of his house and began talking. "Are you going to get an M.B.A.?" I asked.

"Yeah, but I don't really know which school to choose."

"You should go to Cal Berkeley." I could just see how bright his future was and I wanted to be a part of it. I wanted him to make as much money as possible. We came into the house while his mom (who I had an incident with at Lisa's) made dinner for us. We sat at the table and I was desperately trying to not act crazy. Joe was doing his homework and I just watched him while giggling to myself.

His sister joined us for dinner. I've had many experiences with his sister. I had attempted to get her as a girlfriend in a mad sort of way, by dishing out love as if we were married. She knew who I was and what I was about. She thought I was crazy. We sat across from each other at the dinner table. All of a sudden I heard her giggle to herself. My irresistible urge to giggle back came out. Simultaneously while eating dinner we both giggled for five straight minutes at nothing. No jokes were said and there wasn't even conversation. I don't know, and I'm sure she doesn't know, what was funny, but it was laughter from the heart. It was a mind-boggling experience that is hard to achieve. We connected in the strangest of ways. If I had to pinpoint what all the laughter was about I guess we both laughed at how ridiculous my behavior was towards her (all the love I gave) and how it was just insane for me to randomly show up and eat dinner with her.

I was done with dinner, thanked his mom and said to Joe, "Let's go to California University tonight."

It was random but he was an outgoing guy and said, "Okay, but give me an hour or two."

I did not have time for that. I had a destiny to fulfill. "Well, just meet me there," is what I said. I wanted Joe and Jim both to witness me die. At the time I felt they were the most important people in my life. I thought the whole time that Joe knew that I was going to kill myself, when in reality he had no idea what was in my head, but he would remember everything later. Not having any sense of what was real and unreal, I asked, "Can I suck your dick?" in an unnatural way.

"No, you're weird," Joe replied. I thought nothing of it and left. While driving to the University I felt as though every car I passed knew what I was going to do. I felt love all around me. I was thinking such crazy stuff that I can't even describe it now. I thought of how being genuinely crazy is something that only a few people who had ever lived can witness. I was a brick in a wall. I felt in touch with history throughout time and how I was unique, but very real part of it. I could not handle this all at once; I had to pull over for a breather. None or ten cars pulled over next to me. They were glued to me. I was scared. *Now I know this is real.*

I just continued driving. I had not even told Jim I was coming to his house, but I knew he'd be there. I had to find his house all by myself, in a tremendously in stable condition. I thought I could find it because I'd been there three of four times but I got lost. I went to a payphone and reached Jim. "Hello" said Jim.

I could only say one thing, "Jim, I'm going to kill myself." Within seconds I heard ambulances rushing nearby places. People were already killing themselves. "Jim, I'm lost, how do I get there?" I asked and he told me in a calm voice the directions. The thing that stuck me was the fact that the cross street, has the word gay in it, so it rang a bell. "Oh yeah, now I know where it is."

In confusion I arrived at his house and saw Jim at the balcony as though he was John F. Kennedy. He looked intelligent and charismatic, like someone who is capable enough to become president. Jim's girlfriend was home with him. I walked to the table and sat and tried to explain myself. This would be my last story and I would be satisfied with it being over.

"I'm going to kill myself," I repeated three or four times. "I have sex with people and call them shit." They were seated with open ears to hear me out and reason with me. "And Matthew Sheppard (the gay man who was murdered_ was killed because of me."

"Ali, that was in Missouri," Jim said. I continued to cry as the two asked questions. "Ali, can you never be happy?" Jim asked.

"I truly can never have the same chemical balancing as a normal happy person," I told them.

I had forgotten all about my parents. I had to call for a final talk. "Ali, where are you?" my dad asked.

"I'm at California University with Jim, I'm going to kill myself."

"No Ali, we'll do anything you want, name it."

"Dad, I'm crazy, I don't have a brain." I started swinging in the air in front of Jim and his girlfriend to show them I could only do physical movements, with no mental activity. I felt like nothing. I was having a nervous breakdown.

"Ali, we'll come and pick you up." From this point on, Jim and his girlfriend were in another room tapped into my conversation.

"Ali, we'll come and pick you up." From this point on, Jim and his girlfriend were in another room tapped into my conversation,

"Dad, this is my whole plan. Back as a little kid, locked up, I planned that once I reached adulthood, and did everything I could to the world, I would go out a legend." However, there was more damage to be done. My dad couldn't talk any sense to me so he gave the phone to my mom. "I'm going to kill myself," I said. She heard this and laughed. She knew me and she knew it was going to happen; she saw no objective reason for me to do it. To this day there is still no reason why I or anyone else should kill themselves. I didn't want to listen to her.

Okay, I thought, *all I have to do is find a way to end it and do it now*. The cops knocked in the door two seconds later. There were two of them. A friend who I called earlier worked at a police station, and told the cops to go check Jim's house out. *Shit! I'm too late*. The cops told me to come with them. I had a blank look on my face; they almost laughed and I had no choice but to go with them. I felt I had to be killed. *I wasn't successful but I'm sure they will find a way to kill me*. It gave me relief. I was put in an ambulance and driven to a medical center.

Chapter 11

I was thinking of all my old friends whom I had hurt, and how some of them told me to kill myself. I was thinking of all my old friends whom I had hut, and how some of them told me to kill myself. It was all coming out. I could now only speak repressed thoughts. I was checked into the hospital and sent to a room to sit on a chair. My mom and dad drove to the medical center, and saw me. A doctor walked in and the three looked at me with sympathy. "I'm crazy, I hurt so many people, I need the death penalty."

No answer was given. The doctor began giving me sanity test. "Subtract 7 from a hundred 10 times." I did this, no problem. "Recite the alphabet," no problem. "What's your name, where do you live?" Again, I answered with no problem. *Why am I crazy? I can do anything a normal person can do.*

Was I making myself crazy to develop some kind of meaning for my life? What constitutes a crazy person? Is it all in the eye of the beholder? One must keep in mind that life is what your beliefs are, and what you make of it. Maybe I only needed classes in psychology. Maybe all I had to do was try for a good life like most people and things would come together.

I was being driven to a Mental Hospital. I was seated with someone across from me in a van. We both started to laugh. He was laughing at me and I was too. *What a joke people can make of life.* No words were exchanged, only laughter. I actually felt human for connecting with someone. I arrive at the hospital and everyone was doing his or her own tasks. I was then out in a bed with the door shut, and all I thought of was how I needed the death penalty. I thought of all the people who loved me. I thought of how I was different from everyone else. I thought of the insane laughter that I let so many people experience. I had no place on Earth.

The morning came by and I was still laughing, I could not stop. It was uncontrollable laughter at how I ruined the world. It was the same laughter I did in the institution I was put in as a kid. Nothing had changed. From the day you're born and when language is learned, the reality that God has given you is there. It cannot change. The only thing that can change is mood. Who you are is a gift from God. For some reason I am everything. Psychiatric medicine does minimal changes.

I tried to make myself stop laughing. So many thoughts were running through my mind. I heard Jim's voice say, "Ali, if you remember anything, it's that you can't kill yourself." I also felt the feeling of happiness in the air outside of me. "Yes, Ali's not here," is what I thought people were thinking. "The world is so much more peaceful now."

Finally, after a few hours, I gained control over my laughter. That is when a doctor came in. He asked me general questions of how I was feeling, my thoughts and so on. "I need the death penalty," I told him as I recalled the film Dead Man Walking and how the story ended with Sean Penn getting death for his murders. I thought the film's purpose was to make realize that that's how the world wanted me to go. "I'm crazy, I don't have a brain!"

"What have you done? He asked.

I have sex with people and call them shit."

"Would you be able to do this to me?" he asked.

"If I want to."

"Anything else?" he asked. I couldn't think of anything. In reality however I was not ready to die. I still had some love for myself.

The reality around me was confusing. I was like a lost dog. Maybe this was all one big trip in my head. Nevertheless, the repressed thoughts kept coming out one at a time. Once the idea of my being crazy had disappeared, I went to the next level and thought I was evil. The thought of being evil is utter hopelessness. I thought of Habib and how he said he was evil. I thought of how there are many of us evil people, put here solely to commit evil acts. I was reaching rock bottom of how psychotic I could be.

The hospital had playtime where groups are formed to construct things. The groups of patients were playing with glue, paper, and scissors, making designs for fun. I stood still, watching them with a blank look, as lifeless as could be. One girl started to cry, she never knew of that reality. It was scary to her. Life can so "real" that it's scary. She was raped of her happy mod, and experienced nothingness. "Go sit and play with them," a female counselor said.

I shook my head no. She repeated, "Go play."

"I need the death penalty," I said. She did not say anything. I thought I could maybe receive it by how serious I was and I quickly said a statement that meant "I love you." She gave a dark look ad I knew I was not truly serious. If I were I would eventually beat it. I am one of the few people in this world that can beat the death penalty. Not by trial but by love. No one can pull the lever; my love is too strong of a force. It is out of my control. I wish I could stop it because it scares me. Most people hate me for it.

"You're no god!" I heard someone yell out of nowhere. During my stay I was given no special impression that all these things were lies. Now as I look back, most of them could be lies, I have no idea. I went on with whatever came to my head.

I was out on "suicide watch," so someone would watch me 24 hours a day. I tried to sleep so I could give myself a little relief for my stress. At the end of the first night a counselor woke me and asked how I was feeling. I was miserable. "Is there anyone you would like to see?" The two most important people to me at that moment were the ones who best fit the "Survival of the Fittest" theory.

I was barely conscious because of the stress but I manages to say, "My plastic surgeon, and Anthony." I was scared to talk to anyone because I thought I would kill him or her. I could no longer experience any emotional feeling. Sleep gave me the feeling of death, and it all I wanted to do. Every thought was telling me to die, but IO was still stupid. What was going on? The only thing that kept me going was the thought of death, but there was more ahead.

I was woken up and in front of me were my parents and Anthony. Anthony had actually stopped whatever he was doing and had driven himself to see me. I stood up in front of them and half of the floor couldn't help but to look at what was happening. I first glanced at my dad, then my mom. They only had a look of love. Then I saw

Anthony, "Ali, I'm gay." At the time it meant nothing to me. I couldn't say anything to him or my parents due to the stress. The real world was too much for me. I was prey to failure, crying with pain. I could do something else but leave the scene and Anthony entered the room. He put his hand on my shoulder with care, like the Godfather would do, as if to say everything would be all right. I loved him; he made me feel a little better.

Time passed and I only slept and ate—I ate a lot. I was starting to notice that I gaining weight. I distanced myself from everyone in the hospital, so as to not inflict pain on anyone. I thought my life's purpose was to kill everyone I'd come in contact with, until there was no one left. I imagined myself in ten years at a local supermarket with no one being around to shop, because I had killed them all. Fear would make up the atmosphere. I would never stop the rampage, because I had no control. I was Satan.

I was lying on my bed, when a psychologist spoke to me. I was trying my hardest to talk to her with no love. Every question she asked was followed by a long silence, as I thought of words that had no love. "Why are you taking so long to answer me?" she asked.

"I don't' want to hurt you." I felt the good person inside of me, and the devil colliding. The devil was stronger, he was immortal, and he was captain. Everyone has the devil inside of him or her but for some reason mine is the meanest. I love the real me, the good me. "There is a good person inside of me," I said in agony. "How can I kill myself, there is a good person?" I felt that this was impossible. This is why I cannot kill myself. I remembered as a kid when a gun was placed next to me in my cell. I just couldn't do it.

"Is this your first stay in a mental institution?" she asked.

"Yes," I said. Maybe it was. This erases everything I believed in. My life's a lie; I'm not a supernatural being. I was in pain for no reason. At the time I thought as if there was no way they'd let me out. I was to be locked in the institution until they found a way to kill me. I thought that they had previously stuck a gun somewhere in the room so I would find it and do the right thing, which is to kill myself. A male housekeeper entered the room. I thought that he must have been through tremendous tests just to be in that room. I felt there was no way anyone could find a way to kill me. I could outsmart anyone. I had power over the whole world, and I felt lie shit.

"What are you thinking right now?" she asked.

"The other person," I was referring to the housekeeper.

"Jeese," he said, "What did I do?" I thought he was trying to kill me and I wouldn't let it happen. I kept hearing Jim's voice telling me all the facts. Perhaps if I knew none of this, I wouldn't have held the devil as far back as I did, and an exorcism might have been needed, just to calm me down.

A day or so passed and I cooled down and had an interview with a psychologist. I tried to explain how I was evil. I dissected every thought of the devil in me, and tried to show him he was really there, and that I was the only one. "That's the downside of human consciousness. I was a normal person making myself crazy. I tried to beat myself solely for the fact that I had capability. It has been researched that there are at least 30,000 people like me, who feel and think thoughts of the devil like I do, and a milder devil is inside all of us. I was not. Of them, maybe two are truly possessed. I was not. You just can't give the devil control. We choose our own reality. One usually chooses to happy.

Some time passed, and I cooled down again. There was lady who looked after me for a few days to watch me so I wouldn't kill myself. She was a quite lady, pretty, and in her 30s. She only said something if it was not necessary. After taking some of the strongest medication prescribable to get me in reality. "You're not crazy," she said lovingly. I looked up at her, and my heart started to pound. She gave me a sexy look and if I wanted sex at that moment I could have had it. But that would of have been insane. She walked away. A similar situation with a man happened, and there was no sexual attraction. I was at the core of myself, and in the real world for a couple hours.

Visitors and family friends came to see me night after night. "Ali, none of this stuff ever happened, it's ridiculous."

My friend who I grew up with said, "Ali, I was at that party, it never happened." The beliefs of all these thoughts were so real to me that I did not believe him. *It did happen*, is what I thought; I couldn't hide anymore, and act normal. The thoughts were taking over my life. Many of my true friends also called on me in my time of crisis. I found that one, however, whom I grew up with, was a phony friend. The only reason he called was because he felt obligated, not because he cared. I could tell he wanted for me to end my life, so he could forget about me and live his loser life. He was the one who told the cops where I was the night at California University. On the outside he tried to show what little affection he had towards me, but I know love, and on the inside, all he had was hate. He hated the fact that I called him gay.

Everyone else who had telephoned me cared for me. Even after trying to kill everyone, most of my friends still showed affection. I guess they realized it was a time of crisis that I was going through and they forgave me for my actions. After all, I was in the institution, I was crying out for help.

"Ali, what the fuck?" my Australian friend said, referring to my stay in the institution.

"I'll be here forever," was my response. I felt there would be no one who could help me. I then started to think even farther into myself, I thought as though I had been here before. This was the fifth or sixth time I had come. Each time I would start a new disease that would kill millions, like the bubonic plague. However, now I thought I started AIDS, the disease started right around the time I was a couple of years old. "I fucked a monkey in the rainforest, and started the disease." I remembered the situation where I spotted a monkey and knew he was infected with something. I grabbed it out of a selection of twenty, fucked it, and felt as though I injected heroin, heroin to give to everyone. I felt as though the first mission of my life had been completed.

"You're crazy!" my dad's friend said laughing. I gave out an evil laugh, as my dad just stood there with no comment. I was his son, he could not think badly of me. I started to think I had given AIDS to all my friends, and how everyone was on the "Cocktail treatment," and how on TV all they talked about was AIDS, and that I should get a test and stop infecting people with it. I told a psychologist all of this. She could only listen to the insanity I was talking. Blood was taken from me, and I was tested for the disease. The results came out negative.

This was shocking. I had to rationalize it so my stories were true. "They just said I was negative because if they told the truth, I would kill myself, and more people would die." I believed this to be true, no one could save me from my pain, incurable insanity. One black person my age was very kind to me; we played checkers together, and barley talked. His name was Cliff. He was the only real friend I'd met at the institution.

After two weeks of being in the institution I said, "Let me out, I want to go home." Without any trouble I was sent back home. My feelings were that I'd just been through a lot, but still didn't know what the problem was. I was still in the dark. I returned to all of my classes at U.S.C., and I wanted to drop all of them but I stuck it out for about a week. My Business Communication teacher (smartest woman in the world) tried to get a hold me three times during my times or crises, and I avoided her like a coward. I still to this day dream of what she would have told me. Perhaps nothing, as this whole book could be just one big delusion. Would she still hold that love for me and marry me? I am confident that, before the day I die, I will see her again. I have a feeling in my heart that she is for real.

I now, however, do not stress about whether these events "really" happened, but they didn't I experienced everyone in my head as if it were all real. What a reality I was given, true or false. I remember talking to Habib, telling him, "I missed a few weeks."

Without letting me finish, he said, "I spoke to your father already."

I was thinking, right as he said that, *Did you... He is evil*, I thought. But he was evil and smart. That was why he was where he was.

During that time, I was in an outpatient program in Los Angeles. On the way there one time, my dad and I stopped for breakfast at a crowded restaurant. Seated next to me were three average Joes talking. I heard on say deliberately in a joking manner, "These are good pancakes, the best pancakes in the world!" He almost chocked as he said this, as though my presence scared him. I knew he said that because that was the silly way I interpreted things in the world.

I got up to go to the restroom and everyone stared at me. I put my head down, thinking, *I can't do this anymore*. "Bye, bye," two different people said. I thought, *Wow, everyone here knows who I am. Is it the same for everywhere I go?*

Today I think it is, however, they don't care. They live their lives happily; I might be on the back of their minds, but they move on. This is what I hated; I always wanted people to only think about me. People can love, and hate me, but they still aren't crazy, they live their lives.

I came home after an outpatient day at eh institution and hung out with an intelligent friend who I respected very much; his name was Derek. We played basketball. “Ali, did you find out what it was?” referring to my last months’ incidents.

“No.” I said. I still didn’t know what was going on. “Basketball would be fun to watch,” I said.

“Yeah and there’s a lockout,” he said, insinuating that both he and I knew it was due to me. There was a lockout in 1998; the players and the businessmen could not come to an agreement of how to handle operations. I was in the mental hospital in 1998, when it all happened. I was at the point where I was gradually trying to kill myself mentally. The love of the NBA was apparent towards me. “Yes,” they must have thought, “we are too stupid, he is tight, we can’t come to an agreement, so why do we do it? It doesn’t make sense if we’re not all as smart as each other.” I was at such a low point in 1998 that they couldn’t play.

I was treating him like someone that I wanted to like me. “740 IL BMW,” I pointed. No answer from Derek, I wanted there to be absolutely no confusion in hanging out with him. No asking the question, “Why?”

“Ali you’re…” I laughed and didn’t let him finish. As the night ended he started to blab away about nothing I found important. He basically said, “I like you.” That was as much as I could handle at that moment. He, however, played all his cards right, and I thought of him as a true friend.

Chapter 12

It was time for me to take over, and carry out my Grand Plan. "My back hurts." I said.

"Ali, let's go to Mexico," my dad almost demanded. "Farsheed will come with us. We'll pick him up along the way. His store isn't doing good business at the moment."

Once I'd make an appearance there, things would turn around. "Okay," I said, "What about his brother Mazi?"

"He said his back hurts," my dad replied. We are all interconnected, in some way, and I am the master. These two people were the "Fittest" of my dad's friends. I loved them very much.

Palos Verdes was as crowded as I'd ever seen it. Jammed, congested, everyone was leaving town. Perhaps they wanted to join me in Tijuana, where I would reign. My dad drove to Tijuana, where I couldn't make it halfway to San Diego (2 hours) without pulling over. My dad pulled the car over and I immediately cried, as I stepped out of the car and hugged him. "Dad, why me?" I had eaten something and felt a little better. While taking a turn driving I felt that my dad and I were both taken over by my evil spirit. He couldn't drive the car straight, he lost control, by forces Mazhin and him, and he almost veered off of the road. The car ahead of us started driving in a circle too. We almost crashed into a divider. It felt like a supernatural power that simply took us over. And we all knew it had to do with me. I hated it, however.

We made it to Farsheed's store. I saw his face, and it depicted how I felt, blank. He looked like nobody. I saw someone who had completely hated himself. "Ali, we all go through tough times at your age." We had connected. He said, "Ali, if you find anything in the store you like, take it." I felt as though the whole world was watching us in the store. His business would be rolling gain later. We closed the store for the night and proceeded to Tijuana. The traffic was unbelievable. In the twenty times I'd been to Tijuana since then I'd never seen it a tenth as congested. "It's crowded because it's the first day of Christmas vacation." Farsheed said.

"Yeah," I agreed, I didn't want all of this, and I felt like shit. Farsheed was driving like a maniac. He passed cars within centimeters of hitting them, with the confidence of a god.

"I'm not available for another year!" he said, as though I would be like this forever.

We arrived in Tijuana. I walked the streets and thought to myself, *The world is yours*, a line straight from the movie, *Scar Face*. I actually felt confident. I controlled everyone on the streets. I ruled the whole city. Everyone was there under my wings. We proceeded into a strip bar where it was jammed packed.

"Ali, look at girls and see what God has created," Farsheed would say.

I scoped out the most beautiful one and said, "Dad, I want that one." He got her for me, we went to a hotel and fucked, no money exchanged hands.

"You're from Iran," she said.

"Yeah, how did you know?" I asked. She smiled and had no answer. I walked back to my friends and the club went from complete conversation, to complete silence all at the same time.

"Ali, you hit them all," Farsheed told me in Persian. I finally felt connected with everyone in my terms of thinking. This was what I wanted my whole life, to feel as one with everyone, "Ali, look at that girl." He pointed out a Spanish girl who was beautiful. "Ali, go to bed with her."

I looked at her and she laughed. "Do you want to go to a hotel?" I asked.

"Yes," she said. Something about this girl separated her from others; she was special. She kissed and rubbed me like no other girl has, she made me feel so good, I wanted to return the favor, so I performed oral sex on her. While I was doing it, some very clear thoughts entered my head.

I'm as dumb as a fish, I thought, Fish only go around and mate with other fish. All life started with fish, I should die with fish. I should die between her legs. Then she tightened her legs around me to choke me. It felt the natural thing I should do was give in and die between her legs. Die with pleasure. However, I was still too slow as to think of what was going on, I almost ran out of air, but what do fish do when they're out of water? Try to jump back in. I gasped for air and her plan failed. How had she been trained for this? It was a brilliant idea. How well do some people know me? I lay on my back, and she failed.

"What the fuck," was the look in her face, and she wanted to give in and fuck me.

"No," I said, she was too special. So special to me I didn't want to fuck her. She finished orally. I had up to that point never loved a girl as much as I loved her. She was a girl of religion. She had a cross of Jesus on. "Okay, thank you," I said, I wanted to be with her forever, but I walked away. She laughed like Anthony laughed, when he said, "Why would you care?"

"Who was that girl?" I asked Farsheed. He did not reply but I knew she was special. We left town, and dropped Farsheed off. There it was again, the devil crushing us both down as we said our good byes. I however couldn't kill myself, so I gave energy off for Farsheed to kill himself.

He hugged me up in the air and said, "Ali, I love you." I am going to name my first son after Farsheed, that's how much I love him.

As I got in the car with my dad, I heard some kids saying, "Have fun!" sarcastically. We returned home, and had pulled over to pee on the side of the freeway. I wanted to just jump into the cars' path, but a strong force wouldn't let me. I saw other cars trying to ram into me, but they couldn't—they could sway a second, but their love for me didn't allow them to run me over. I hated myself, and they hated me. There was no way out, or at least so I thought.

I returned the next day to work at Lisa's, I was still in an imbalanced state, and I had to said to the waitress, "I'm going to make a trip to Brazil." In the newspaper the next day the headlines read, "Brazil ready to go to war." I saw this and knew I was affecting the whole world. I had the whole world in my hands.

I had been starting to smoke cigarettes and watched CNN, and the reporter said, "Cigarette smoke is now known to cause impotence." I felt as though he was talking directly to me, like I was one on one with the man, it was scary. If I were to continue to smoke, millions would imitate me and become hooked.

The next day I attended the outpatient program. I had burst out of my bubble of quietness. I became better friends with Cliff, as I described what I felt about all the patients. All of the patients were related to me in one way or another. I had said things like, "Yeah, the one on the dress is the hottest girl here," and, "Oh, the one with the messed up nose, she's okay."

"You don't even remember names?" said Cliff laughing.

"No," I replied. I started talking about which Mercedes I liked best. He listened. We had group and I came out even more. "How can you live with the idea that someone else is better at something than you?" I asked.

"I know there are smarter psychologists than me, but it doesn't bother me," a man named Rick said.

"Yeah, but if someone's better than you it makes you sad."

"Why?" another psychologist named Guy said, with hate and confusion.

I had no response. As I write this novel today my attitude has changed to a "Who cares" attitude. I don't think of "the best." I try to be happy.

Other people in the group started to talk. "I have no place on this Earth," one lady said, who I now remember meeting as a kid. I saw the best basketball player who at the time was the one that I got to at a young age. He always looked worried, and had the expression of fear and of "Why are you doing this?" They brought a girl who had the "lowest self-esteem" in. I was talking away for the first time in the institution, making no sense in anything I said.

Lunch came, and I sat next to Cliff, and a girl named Rosa. "I want to marry you," said Rosa. I was the most lovable person in the world. What girl wouldn't want someone who has no personal complaints, and lets the girl take charge? I had a blank head, so she could talk about anything with me, and I would just agree with what she said.

The next day at lunch was different because I was feeling depressed. I saw a variety of food to choose from, and I said, "I'll have the fish." Everyone around me laughed.

"With teriyaki sauce?" the chef said, already knowing what I liked.

"Yeah." I ate it and said to myself, *This is who I am. Admit it Ali, you're a* fish. I was again beating myself up. I looked in the corner of my eye and saw Rick bobbing his head up and down in the air, imitating a fish out of water.

Cliff sat next to me, "My joints ache. Why is that?" My first thought was coming out saying, *Because you're bla…., no, that's not why*, I quickly tried to be good. "Why is that?" he said again.

"I don't know," I said. How did he already know me? He knew me in such a short time.

"Do you remember what that big guy said when he came in here?"

I tried to remember, whom, and it came to me, Anthony. "No, I don't remember," I replied, almost crying every word I said.

"He said he was gay. What do you think of that?" he asked.

"I'm straight!" he said, "Why would you ask such a question?" I had no response. He started to speak to me. I could tell he loved me. He wanted to know more about who I was. I was interesting to him, and had established a friendship. "I'm in here because I hit my girlfriend," he said. "Would you it your girlfriend?" he asked with curiosity.

"We all have our problems," I said.

"Yeah, but would you hot her?"

What the hell does this guy want from me? I thought. "We all have our problems," I repeated, and I thought, Where's my mom, she should be here soon. I walked away from Cliff while he was talking to me; just wandered off to see if my mom had come to pick me up, without saying a word to Cliff. I could not find her, and group session was going to begin again. For some reason I saw Cliff crying to the psychologists alone. I went to the bathroom later and heard Cliff crying, "Cliff what's wrong?" I asked.

"Ali, I don't know if I'm going to make it through today," he said crying,

"Why?" I asked, as he kept crying. "Is there something you guys aren't telling me?"

"No Ali, it's not you, you'll be alright," he said. "I'm not going to make it past tonight," he continued, crying his eyes out.

"What are you doing later?" I asked.

His tears stopped, "Nothing."

I knew it was all because of me, and if I started to hang out with the guy it wouldn't all be over. "Ali, you go play ball with your tough friend." He knew me, and how I love the strongest people. We both walked out. "Guy" held me back.

"No, I can help him," I said.

"Ali, you leave this job up to us." I was ready to call them shit, but I calmed down and went to group where we were told to write down what we were thinking.

"All people should be loved, black, white, Asian, or any color, gay or straight. Survival of the fittest is a crock of shit." I was stopped from reading.

"It's not a crock of shit. I'm fit," said a female psychologist. All my beliefs were colliding, and I was in no way certain what I was going to do with my life. I didn't know what to do in five minutes.

"I need the death penalty."

"I agree." Another person said.

"All the problems you people talk about, like not having enough money, or a situation going bad, are not real problems." I said, as though I was God enlightening them. The next person was speaking of their problems when I saw the smartest looking guy in the world.

He told me, "We haven't spoken yet." We had gone to a booth where it was only the two of us speaking to each other, and a wheel chair with a straight jacket right next to me in case I got crazy. I said something that was the equivalent to saying I don't like myself.

"Why?" he asked. This was why the straight jacket would have been needed, if I had tried to kill him by showering him with love, as I have so many smart people in the past. I had no response. This guy was one of the smartest people in the world, and knew me better than I knew myself. I bet he has been analyzing me since day one of my mischief.

"I killed the dinosaurs," I said. He shook his head "okay" and wrote it down. "And Cliff…"

He interrupted, "We're not supposed to talk about this, but why is that?"

"Because he loved me!" I screamed, "He didn't know that was possible."

"Okay," he shook my hand and knew I was going to go crazy. The straight jacket wasn't used. I calmed myself down. What happened to Cliff, and why? Now as I look back, he thought he had a relationship with me. He had love for me, and when I walked away from him to check up on my mom, his whole idea of love and what it stood for crashed. Love was nothing any more. He could no longer love anyone again because, "Who cares?"

I didn't care for him; love to me is for the most part unreal. Why would I care? Is what I thought. Love is what most people live for, and to be raped from the ability to love someone else is the equivalent of losing your soul.

Group ended with what the patient was going to try on over the course of the next day. "I will have a positive day, and think about fish." Like a bullet, "And go fish," said Guy.

"Yes." It was startling to come together. I stood outside as the master psychologist started his car. He uncontrollably ran his car into the speed bump, before hitting reverse. This scared me, he had all the mind power in the world, and I could still cause him to lose control. My mom came, and I told her, "Mom, let's go fish. Okay? But Mom, what is it? Is there something you're not telling me?"

"No Ali," I still did not have that final piece, but I knew going fishing would clear things up. Boom it hit me, this is my last day on the planet, and it was not because of other people trying to kill me, it was myself who was the enemy, and me who had to end it.

I came home and the night arrived, I brought my Chihuahua and my mom to the local shopping center. "I'm as dumb as a fish, and all fish do is mate with other fish and leave them." I said.

"Do you see us any different from anyone else?" (Us, referring to my family) she asked.

"No." I recall her asking the same thing in a similar situation at the age of four, nothing had changed except for my age. "And my plastic surgeon…" I said.

She interrupted, "Why did you do it?" referring to the sex. I walked past the local pizza place where my sister had worked, and saw them all doing their normal jobs, and the next second complete silence. As though I had "Hit" them all.

I came home and was practicing yoga with my mom because I had nothing else to do. My friend from junior college called, “Ali, there’s a party in Torrance, do you want to drink and go?”

I answered, “I don’t drink anymore.”

“Is this Ali?” he said confused.

“Yeah, I stopped drinking.” I hung up on him, and watched my mom do the dishes; the question of why I am here was now as great as it had ever been in my life. My mom almost cried doing the dished and couldn’t finish. She was experiencing my world.

My dad, smart as he is, stayed calm, “Here Ali, read this.” It was John Steinbeck’s, The Tortilla Flat. It was one of the greatest books ever written. I knew this, I was reading it out loud, and there was nothing else to do. I only heard words, no meaning, while reading the book. I heard my dad laugh as if, “Who is he reading to?”

They were just blank words, until I read, “The fish he had caught,” then two lines later, “and the brandy.” That was it. “Ahhhh. My accounting teacher, I love him, I’d die for him.” I hugged my dad helplessly. With less meaning, “My Communications teacher, my Organizational Behavior teacher, Jim.” The whole time I could feel Habib with me. I felt as though he was telling me to do the right thing, to kill myself. It was the strongest force I had ever felt.

“Ali, let’s go take a walk,” my dad said. All I could feel outside was the question *Why?* We could not even make it up the street, because we heard cars crash. I was too scared to see what had happened. I walked by every house, and occasionally heard a gun shit. “Bye, Bye,” I heard. *Wow, I really have to do something*. One of my neighbors couldn’t drive up the street without stopping, due to feeling deep love. My sister didn’t come home from work, because she was keeping all her co-workers under control.

My dad and I came back inside and went on the internet; however, it was so congested that we could not find the information my dad wanted to show me. It was something about “Intangible Assets.” Even today I have no idea why he wanted to show me that. Perhaps it had something to do with Habib. So instead we looked at pornography.

I was just waiting around thinking of nothing until a powerful thought came: *I want to kill myself.* It was the good person inside of me giving up, letting the devil completely take over. It was very real. I gave up. I was hating myself every second, I was only asking myself the question, *Why? Why would I go to bed tonight?* Is what I thought. This is where I should have said, "Dad, I want to go fish." That was the only way to go. Jump in the water and be with the fish. The world was ready to see what I'd do. This is where I had the most power in the world. A decision to be made that would affect the world more than the most important of decisions a president could ever make. Was I going to kill myself? If I were to go fish, a revelation would have taken place, and the population today would not have reached 6 billion as soon as it did. "Dad, I want to go to bed." I said---why, I don't know. He laughed, and also thought, *why?*

Chapter 13

This was the point where I would gradually lose all my power. My Grand Plan had failed to come through, all of the things that I did were meaningless. The next day all I would be able to do was urinate, and eat, as a fish does, no other thought could enter my head. I thought I would kill myself, that day.

"I'm going to go fish," I told my so-called friend.

"With you dad?" ha sked, advising me that he wanted for e to kill myself. *Is this person my friend?* I went and on the way there I saw a big California University blanket, hanging from a person's apartment. This was supposed to make me feel bad, because of the way I treated Jim.

I took the Tortilla Flat with me and tried to read it again. I couldn't find the word fish or brandy. What the fuck? It was all in my mind. I remember Jim saying, "Ali, if you remember anything is that you can't kill yourself." I saw some smiles on people's faces for not killing myself. I couldn't bring myself to do it.

"Truman, jump in the water!" an average looking Joe said to me, laughing. I just laughed back. Maybe The Truman Show showed

Truman's last scene in the water, so subconsciously I knew I had to go fish.

I had told my sister, "I'm crazy, and I'll just be a specimen for others to watch." I was at Lisa's later that night and no waitress would show up to work. They were all scared of me. One church-goer who was extremely religious came and treated me as if I were a friend. Another worker that I liked worked. I had called a couple of friends to come work for me, and I could hear they were crying. As if to say, "If Ali kills himself, I'll kill myself." A lady sat in the back of the restaurant talking on her cellular phone, as if I were a specimen she was watching. I told the manager not to schedule me to work anymore.

I was so overcome with fear that I have my parents sleep in the same room as me. One night all I heard my dad do is laugh, as I laughed also about what I did to the world. As I fall asleep, I almost felt the walls and roof breaking, as all of my energy was given off. As in the movie *The Exorcist*, I could hear objects cracking as I concentrated so hard. I heard the sky rumble if I let my mind go blank. I thought I was the anti-Christ.

My days later consisted of eating, playing basketball, and renting movies. I would later gain all the friends I had hurt in the past back. There are some people that will never forgive me; I still care for these people. Remember, forgiveness is a gift that God has given us. I became a better person and got my job at Lisa's back. I was talking to people on the same wavelength; I had been hitting on girls.

Today, I feel normal. I don't know how I went so long in the dark. I'm not stupid. I'm not evil. My diagnosis today is major depression with psychotic thoughts. This explains my whole story. I was just an unhappy person, who fantasized about everything. I do have a future, and most of the time I don't even think I'm crazy.

People who are truly crazy and like themselves, I do not understand. Everyone you talk to just wants to hit you in the face and tell you to shut up. You are not on the same level of intellect as the average person, and cause trouble.

The confidence level that most crazy people achieve is usually powerful and strange. No one else can match it. Adolph Hitler killed others in order to achieve his sense of confidence. My confidence today comes from God. Believing in God has made me feel normal. It is impossible to find true love, because crazy people are not like anyone else. One must deny the truth, and struggle in order to fit in with others, while not being happy. Illegal drugs only make matters worse. Sometimes it feels as though a boxer is mentally hitting at me, and I lose the true happiness that I worked so hard to achieve. I stay away from drugs, but feel drinking is okay in moderation.

In the past I remember hating myself, in order to be liked by the other person, with no respect for myself. A balance is the solution. What a single person is capable of thinking in life is amazing. No more bad doings, stealing, drugs, being stupid. I have found God. My purpose in life is to live a positive life for him. Good is more powerful than evil and always triumphs in the end. I'm beginning to love myself, and love the Lord. If one thing is certain, it is that God does love me, and forgives me for what sins I've committed.

What is it? I used to think. "It's" faith in God, that there is a higher energy source than us. I have let Jesus Christ into my life, and hope to someday reach eternal happiness. God gives true confidence, and can lead to true happiness, unlike drugs that give you temporary happiness and a false sense of confidence. I still see nothing wrong with having a few beers to unwind every now and then. Today I'm not even capable of being stupid like I was. I have tried to go back, and think of things like I did "before," but it's not the same. I can never go back. I can't talk "Queer" anymore; I can't hate myself as I did before.

I have really changed into a whole new person. Believe it or not, most the time I think that I'm normal. Slip-ups happen all the time, and when they do they are not as bad as before. I think now, *how could I live with myself before? How could I keep the sheared so long?* I find it funny. But in reality it's nothing to laugh at. The purpose or writing this book is to get closure. The negative thoughts are overwhelming. *I can't be stupid forever, and accept who I am*. I want to now forget the past, what might or might not have happened, and live my life. I want to be somebody.

Pure love is an amazing thing, it is the most powerful force that people have. I spent the first eighteen years of my life giving it to as many people as I could, and later destroyed every personal relationship I had, while hoping that when I died everyone would follow with me. I wanted to start a revelation. I couldn't resist having that kind of power. My plan was to kill myself, and laugh at the world, for being the weak person that I am. Obviously, I did not kill myself, and I now have an interesting story to tell everyone. I am just now (at age 23) starting to find my true self. I now pursue true happiness. I no longer play with love as I did before. I have for the most part held myself back, and am proud of myself for doing do. Forgiveness and acceptance are what I am now searching for. Obviously not everyone will forgive me for the things that I have done, but the people that do, I respect.

Epilogue

Well, thank you for reading my book and I hope you are still sane afterward and have learned some things without being too angry, or exhausted.

No other book has been written like this one, and I have plenty more coming. I'm HIV negative after my 50 hookers and countless sexual encounters—so, thank god.

My second book is written from a present day perspective, and I cover everything from serial killers to love and compassion. I love writing and I appreciate you reading my novel.

My new home is soon to be in beautiful Costa Rica. Depending on my success, I hope to live with some friends and write on the beach. I survived my disease and whatever yours might be, if you have one, live—who cares; fuck them. Life is your natural right, and don't let yourself or anyone else take that away from you.

Writing this book gives me great closure on my past and it helped me deal with my friendships and yet remain somewhat good. I don't regret writing the book because now I can put some things behind me. I'm sure there are a countless number of other stories worth telling, better than mine, and I encourage you to write them, also.

Please understand I don't want to be known as a bad person or to bring shame to anyone. I always intend good, but I'm a little unaware of my surroundings and that's when bad happens. Remember me someone who never gives up and who wants to be happy. But it's rather difficult to get it right in this lifetime.

I hope you were able to appreciate the full experience of reading the book—by smiling and being a little confused, and also able to help yourself a little. Use the information I give in a good way, love your brother! Don't ruin the world as I have made myself out to have done. Today all the thoughts of these terrible actions I speak of are fading. Most say the thoughts are not rue and I'm happy to put this book out to help figure out some things.

God Bless,

Ali

Made in the USA
Monee, IL
08 November 2026

67983957R00083